This is a love story. In *Such Precious Clay* you find out why even the most genuine earthly love between a man and a woman can never be trusted completely until it is empowered and transformed by the love of God. You will also come to know how love so transformed becomes a rock upon which the fiercest waves of trial may crash without effect. If you think you are in love, then you owe to your lover, and to yourself, to read this book together. And this is not a love story for the young alone (though it is surely for them). Having been married more than forty years, I found myself gripped and challenged by the candidly told story of a couple who faced the fearful night that all lovers dread, only to discover their fear turned into gladness, and their dreaded night as bright as the sun. As you hold this book in your hand to read these lines, it may be that God has placed it there...for love's sake.

—**Dennis D. Frey,** Th.D., President
Master's International School of Divinity

The emerging trend in Christianity is to use narrative to tell one's story of faith. This book is more than a love story. What makes this story different is that it is not only a narrative of life experience but an exposition of biblical truth applied a real life experience. Mark has effectively used his and Debbie's story to teach great biblical truths from the very character of God to his ability to meet the deepest needs of life. *Such Precious Clay* should be read not only for its narrative value, but for its biblical exposition. This book will not only touch the heart but it will affect the soul and mind.

—**Gary R. Becker,** D. P. Th.
Founder and President of Biblically Balanced Ministries

I plan on using *Such Precious Clay* as required reading for my Psychology & Theology class at the Alliance Graduate School of Counseling. Mark Grawehr's text is a valuable resource for students as they attempt to formulate their own theology of suffering.

—**Dr. Michael Gillern**
Alliance Theological Seminary

This "love letter" ranks with books like *Tuesdays with Morrie*. His Christmas present to Debbie moved me as few things I have ever read. It is a superb emotional moment, among so many others. *Such Precious Clay* demonstrates how clear it is that his life has the character of fine steel, tempered by suffering, strengthened by faith, and made flexible in experience.

—Eugene Savettiere
Retired Business Executive

What an incredible and truly inspiring story of how two people could be so devoted to one another despite such monumental obstacles. God's work in the Grawehr's lives is obvious, even to those of us in the secular world.

—Scott Smith, P.E.
Vice President, Accuspec Inc.

Such Precious Clay

God's

Handiwork

with

Fragile Vessels

Mark Grawehr

Foreword by Joni Eareckson Tada

Pleasant Word

A Division of WINEPRESS PUBLISHING

Pleasant Word (a division of WinePress Publishing, PO Box 428, Enumclaw, WA 98022) functions only as book publisher. As such, the ultimate design, content, editorial accuracy, and views expressed or implied in this work are those of the author.

Editorial Assistance: Len and Carolyn Goss.
GoodEditors.com

Unless otherwise noted, all Scriptures are taken from the *Holy Bible, New International Version®, NIV®*. Copyright © 1973, 1978, 1984 by the International Bible Society. Used by permission of Zondervan. All rights reserved.

ISBN-10: 1-4141-1351-X
ISBN-13: 978-1-4141-1351-7
Library of Congress Catalog Card Number: 2008906390

ISBN-10: 1-4141-1272-6
ISBN-13: 978-1-4141-1272-5
Library of Congress Catalog Card Number: 2008906390

Foreword

Before You Begin...

THE FIRST TIME I met Mark and his wife, Debbie, I stopped and stared. My husband and I had only been married a short time and I was naturally interested in other couples who possessed that special 'something' which set them apart. I wasn't disappointed in Mark and Debbie.

It was summertime and we were at one of our Joni and Friends Family Retreats tucked away in the beautiful, shady mountains of eastern Pennsylvania. The Grawehrs had arrived early and were unpacking their car. When Ken and I wheeled up to greet them, Mark had just lifted Debbie out of the front seat and was gently placing her in a small, rickshaw-like cart. "Are you comfortable?" he asked, and she answered by blinking her eyes. The severity of her disability was pretty obvious.

Something else was obvious, too. This was a couple who were truly devoted to one another. Later on during the Family Retreat, I was also to learn about their devotion to God. Despite the ravages of advanced multiple sclerosis and the rigorous demands it clearly placed on Mark, this husband and wife team showed no resentment toward God or other couples who seem to have it easier.

Watching these two, I learned that marriage is not a 50-50 proposition; it gives all. I also learned that marital love and commitment truly is possible, no matter how challenging the circumstances. Over the years, this was especially reinforced as Debbie's condition continued to deteriorate, wrecking havoc on her frail body and mind. Yet Mark was unflinching—during the worst of times, he defined what it means to be a godly husband.

But I'm getting ahead of myself. And so are you. There is so much more to this remarkable story—a story that even involves another woman! Trust me, the book you are holding in your hands is definitely a surprising read. More than that, Such Precious Clay will inspire you, challenging your very concept of what it means to obey God, as well as honor your spouse. You will learn about the joy of relationships and the power of prayer, the strength of God's grace, and the miraculous—often mysterious—way He weaves the strangest of circumstances into a life plan we wouldn't trade for the world.

Just ask Mark.

Joni Eareckson Tada
Joni and Friends International Disability Center
Agoura Hills, California

Acknowledgments

—⁂☙—

SUCH PRECIOUS CLAY? Already you may be wondering what such a title can possibly mean.

Well, Jesus often used story to teach much of the wonder of truth. I think he still does. Allow me then, if you will, to share our story during a most special season of our lives. God's all-surpassing power was made known to me personally, in small part and yet in such a real and powerful way, through the life of my beloved wife, Debbie.

I have always been amazed the way God creates, molds, and fires our earthly vessels, revealing his wisdom and purpose. We have had opportunities to share our story with groups large and small, and over the years people who had been close to Debbie and me have encouraged me to tell our story in a wider format—to write a book.

Debbie departed this world over twelve years ago. Now I am at a place where I hope and believe God has much to teach not only me, but many others as well, about his purposes for Debbie Grawehr. I am aware of my own inability to communicate this fully to you, let alone to understand personally the depth of meaning and the full effect of the lessons from that season in my life. But I believe very strongly that God spoke in the life and struggles that Debbie underwent. I also believe that you the reader will find much here to benefit and bless your own pilgrimage.

So, I am rewinding the tape. I am inviting you to witness a journey made by two people who had no idea what lay ahead on the road, and who were often shocked and even more often changed by what they encountered. I have thought and prayed long and hard about the events that I am about to relate. I have to admit that I have mixed feelings about telling you this story. I am excited, yet I feel a return of the emotions that I went through during sixteen years of coping with what turned out to be a deadly illness that dominated our lives and marriage.

Through all of this I came to have a much deeper understanding of God's work and will in our lives, though I also recognize that I will never understand, this side of eternity, all that God has for me in this. I can only hope for continued personal nurture as well as a special touch of comfort and inspiration for you who will read this.

At the forefront of those encouraging me to write this story is my wife Becky. She has given me her full support, refreshed my memories when the details were vague in the mists of the past, and has been both a kind and truthful critic. Becky, I love you.

Joni Eareckson Tada's life and ministry have affected and inspired us beyond measure. I must also acknowledge Chad Brand for his scholarly assistance and the practical and prayerful input and support of our dear friends and family, especially Debbie's Mother Florence.

A final word of acknowledgement, love, and thankfulness:

This memoir is dedicated, in a response of gratitude for
the Holy Spirit's work, to
My Precious Beeba
A Window that God's Light Has Shown Through
A Treasure in a Mere Jar of Clay

We are all lumps of clay. God wishes to transform us into vessels that are more and more Christ-like. In so doing, he makes us into precious clay, precious because the Master Potter himself is such a master workman. And so, I offer this testimony to you that you may grow in the knowledge of him and be blessed as we were.

Contents

_#♮◯_

Introduction

꧁

HAVE YOU EVER played with modeling clay or Play-Doh? No matter what your age, whether you are artistic or not, you were probably exposed to the satisfying experience of taking a ball of clay and molding it into something recognizable, at least to you. Perhaps you even modeled a person's face or shape from the dough.

Think of this experience as a microcosm of God's own creativity. If we take the comparison too literally it will break down, as metaphors often do, but it's a good picture of his work in us. God made man of the dust of the earth, and if you live in a place where clay is the primary component of your soil, you know that clay can blow as a fine dust that clings to your skin. The difference, though, between fashioning a torso and limbs from modeling clay and what God did is that we are making something from something. God made the first man from nothing, in that he created the very dust from which He then created Adam.

The word "clay"— the lump of shapeless dough it first represents and the way it can be formed into something beautiful, though impermanent—offers an apt metaphor for us to understand the work of God. The inspired writers of the Bible often chose clay as a metaphor to represent us. The Old Testament book of Job (10:9) records the anguished prayer of the godly man Job as he tries to understand his miseries: "Remember that you molded me like clay. Will you now turn me to dust again?" The prophet Isaiah calls humanity the clay and God the potter (29:16, 45:9). Much later, the apostle Paul calls believers "jars of clay" (2 Corinthians 4:7).

That's us. We are, indeed, jars of clay, fragile, breakable, finite, and yet beautiful in our uniqueness. Each of us is precious to God, ready to be molded into his glorious image. Our bodies may fracture, shatter, and disintegrate, but we hold the eternal love and treasures of God that will not leach out or evaporate.

The story in this book has God's molding hands all over it. This is not merely our story. Before the Creator of the universe spoke this world into being, this story had already begun. It is a story that began in the heart of God. It is merely my awesome privilege to express how He did an amazing work in a very precious and fragile jar of clay.

My attempt here is to enable you to know something of the story of one of the precious souls you can have the joy to encounter in the eternity to come. It is my prayer—as we journey through a few decades of time together in this little volume—that you will have a fresh vision of the work of the God, who is, as the Bible calls him, the "Master Potter," and that you will be strengthened in ways that will make a difference in your life. I hope you will find yourself bursting with the warmth of a newly-revived faith in God's goodness as you gaze upon the Light that shone through Debbie Grawehr, his broken jar of clay. I trust you will find the rest and joy that Debbie herself experienced as the Potter shaped her little by little and piece by piece into the kind of glorious vessel he wanted. That is the kind of molding that the Master Potter does.

This is the story of a woman who was lovely yet fragile, breakable as a delicate piece of pottery. In the winter of early 1996 my "thirty-eight-years-young" wife lay dying. She was the woman of my dreams. She was the best thing that had yet happened to me, and I knew it from the moment we began dating. Physically, however, in 1996 she was nothing like the dream girl I had married in October, 1979—blond hair, blue eyes, captain of the high school twirlers, and homecoming queen runner-up. That once healthy and beautiful young woman was now physically unrecognizable. Her body had been twisted and contorted in such a way that it was painful for many people even to look at her. She had multiple sclerosis. It had seized control of her system within months of our wedding. In fact, in all likelihood she had it in her body the day we wed, though we did not know it. By 1996 she had fought the illness for so long that some of her joints had calcified as the spasms and contracted muscles no longer allowed even therapy to mitigate. Her illness had been a major part of our life together for almost our entire marriage, and now she was slipping away from me—and there was nothing I could do about it.

I read somewhere that "Debbie" meant "bee," so I endearingly called her "My Precious *Beeba*." She reminded me of a beautiful little bee, always working industriously and effectively to carry out its work. In my youth, I had never thought it possible that I could be so much in love with someone as I was with Debbie. I know it sounds like a cliché, and I often wonder what people mean when they say such things, but it was very clear we really were made for each other. It was just perfect!

So, how do you deal with it when the perfect fit is about to depart from you forever? How do you handle life when it appears that what has become your very reason for existence is being taken from you—and there is not a thing you can do to make it stop? How do you cope with the imminent death of the woman you love when life's dreams have never been realized and only have become, in some ways, a prolonged nightmare?

In my case, of course, I had had plenty of time to prepare for this final destination on Debbie's protracted and painful journey. We had known for a long time that things might very well end up this way with Debbie's illness. It was kind of like being on a runaway train with a long empty track for hundreds of miles ahead. You know that you are going to be challenged along the way, and though you have times when you feel relatively safe from harm, you also know that one day the train will meet another object head on. It might be many miles down the track, but you know it is there, and you know that it will be very, very hard.

I guess in one sense her destiny was no different from anyone else's. As the thirteenth century Scottish patriot William Wallace once said, "Every man dies!" As I watched my beautiful wife slowly deteriorate physically, I knew that she was headed for the same thing all of us are headed for—eventually, death. I will have to face the same prospect myself one day, and so one day will all those I love, if Christ does not return again for his church before that time.

And yet, there is something of a difference here between the two. The difference lies in the clarity and the obvious downward trajectory as the process of dying played itself out. I sense my own aging process more all the time. I don't run the mile quite as sprightly as I used to. It takes me longer to recover from a workout than it did five years ago. I find little aches and pains at times that I did not notice before. Now don't get me wrong. I am not yet ready for a retirement community, and the candles on my cake don't yet cause the temperature to rise in the house on my birthday, but I do sense the aging process slowly moving me toward the inevitable.

With Debbie, the process was different. It was as if her life had been put on fast forward while everyone around her still moved at normal speed. Her once vibrant body was forced to crash its way through rapid deterioration and incapacity until it was finally clear that the end was at hand. That body was frail and fragile clay, but *what precious clay!*

On the surface, this story may seem like a record of one couple's experiences as they faced illness, decline, and death together. But it is not the whole story. You see, while my Precious Beeba's body was racing toward destruction, something else was going on at the same time. Something we never expected the day we found out that she was sick. What we later realized was going on was God had been starting something in our lives. Now I recognize he had been whispering to us for a long time before we ever were conscious of it. That is kind of the way the Lord works—poking around in someone's life, preparing him or her for the day when he shows up *in person* and says, "Here I am. Now what are you going to do about it?" He had been preparing us for a long time for what he was going to do through the process of Debbie's illness. But when he finally did show up *in person*, it was quite a shock.

And it was God walking alongside us—even more than Debbie's illness—that really made the ultimate difference in our lives. Let me take our story back to the beginning—back to the time that the Lord was at work, even though we could not yet recognize him.

Chapter 1

God's Work Begins

—⟨⟩—

The Clay that Formed Debbie

OUR STORY IN the early days was probably like the story many of you could tell—nothing very extraordinary. And this always reminds me that you can't determine the end of a story by its beginning. Most of Charles Dickens's novels were about very, very common people (like Bob Cratchet and Oliver Twist), but common people who were confronted by circumstances they never expected. Then, along the way, they often became larger than life heroes or villains. In Debbie's life story, the early details are important for understanding the way things finally worked out for Debbie and me.

The date was August 24, 1957. William and Florence Winkelman were swelling with joy at what had just been handed ceremoniously to them by the doctor in the delivery room of the hospital that day. In their arms lay their new baby girl, Debbie. They laid her fragile little form in a clean white bassinet, and just stared at her with smiles on their faces, the kind of smile that every parent has when gazing for the first time on his or her new child. Babies speak so hopefully to us. Here is a new life, a life that might make a difference in the world. Here is the picture of innocence sleeping peacefully in our arms. Here is a life that, we hope, will be long and happy. Here is a life so fragile, and yet, all things being considered, no one would even guess that this child might not live out her expected years in happiness and contentment.

No one could have imagined the trauma that would impact this "jar of clay," this "earthen vessel," as the apostle Paul calls it. Nor could anyone imagine the impact she would have on those who knew her, as well as on the myriads of unseen beings observing the Master Potter's plan. This was just a newborn child in a white hospital bassinet, and her parents simply adored her.

Debbie was a good baby who did not tax the patience of Bill and Flo more than they expected. They loved her very much and did what good parents do to try to help their little one prepare for life in the world. Dressed in lace and smiling most of the time, Debbie cooed and chattered her way through her baby years.

Time ticked by—days turning to weeks, weeks to months. Photographs, memories, baby steps, giggles, and all the normal things that happen in normal families around America happened in Debbie's family. Outsiders would not have seen anything particularly unusual about the family, though they would have noted that Debbie was doted on and treasured by her parents. This little girl loved life and loved what she did with life.

She loved her grandparents, "Nana" and "Pop-Pop." Her bright blue eyes looked intently at people, animals, and inquisitively sought to understand what was going on in the world around her. Debbie especially loved animals. "Pete," her little black bunny, especially brought a smile to her cute, chubby face when he was given to her at Easter in 1961. She loved visiting the local zoo so that she could feed the deer and goats, and though she did not really understand the significance of it yet, to enjoy the wonder of discovery and the creativity of the Master Creator. One day, she would be able to understand how God often draws us to himself as we revel in the wonder of his magnificent creation. But that day was far beyond the distant horizon for the little girl who simply loved furry creatures.

Deb's mom Flo tells about Debbie's eagerness to learn. She followed her closely in the kitchen, learning to bake at a young age. A few years after Debbie came into this world, her parents brought home from the hospital a little brother, Glenn. He brought even more joy and smiles to the happy little home, and Debbie enjoyed helping her mom take care of the new little brother. Every year at Christmas Debbie would make a new handmade ornament for the Christmas tree. The Winkelman Christmases were almost like a Norman Rockwell print.

Debbie's family attended a local Catholic church. She knew all of the kinds of experiences that were so common in the world of people who watched *Andy Griffith* and *I Love Lucy* on television. Going camping with the Girl Scouts, wearing skirts to school, playing outside after school with the kids in the neighborhood, dressing up in your very best on Easter Sunday for Mass—these were the regular experiences of Debbie Winkelman. As she grew a little older, Debbie decided she wanted to learn to twirl the baton. She would become very good at it.

Debbie's face emanated a soft, childlike beauty with a mysterious, welcoming smile. She was always popular at school, not just because she was cute, but because she had a winsome yet quiet personality that drew many people to her. Her gentle sweetness and genuine kindness touched many people, even those who barely knew her. Most of her acquaintances quite simply thought of her as a "very special" young lady.

At the football games, many people would cheer, whistle, and holler, encouraging the twirlers on. There was one unnoticed, silent voice, though, whose hardened heart would seem to melt as he watched this all American dream girl from a distance. It would be awhile before he would attempt to shorten that distance.

The Clay from Which I Was Formed

My parents' families came from two completely different worlds. My father's family had been among the aristocracy back in the old Swiss/Austrian world. This was the world of pride, prestige, old money, with links back to the even older world of the ancient Roman Empire. People from that heritage are often raised to believe that they have a purpose to represent and preserve the glory of what was once a great and glorious achievement—the beauty and power of ancient and medieval European culture.

My mother's family, on the other hand, was from a Slovak/Polish background. Their cultural practices and ethnic characteristics could not have been more different from those of my father's ancestors. For centuries the families who could trace their lineage back to ancient Roman and Greek cultures regarded the Slovaks, who could not, as a lower people than they were. The attitude even colored the political climate—as late as the 1930s Adolf Hitler made the Slovaks his number-two target, right after the Jews.

Thus my mother and father were formed from different clay, we might say. But in America, of course, the distinction between the ancient aristocracy and peasantry has generally faded away. So when my father and mother met, they did not see themselves as coming from different worlds, but from the same world—New Jersey. My parents are wonderful salt-of-the-earth people, the kind of people who have made America great. My father had to leave my mom, his new wife, just days after they were married to serve our country in the military in Korea. Not until after his tour of duty, about two years later did he return home to reunite with his bride to start a family. In other words—I was born, on June 10, 1957. My dad went to work to build a comfortable home life for his wife and future children. He decided to go to dental school. He went to school during the day, worked nights, and even delivered pies in order to keep food on the table during those lean and difficult school years.

My family eventually moved from Jersey City to the suburbs of Montville and I attended the new Catholic school there. We belonged to the Roman Catholic faith, and Catholics often attempt to integrate faith and education by sending their children to parochial schools. This is still very common in some parts of the country. At first our church met in a barn. If your only impression of Catholics is that they all go to beautiful and ornate church buildings, I can tell you that sometimes that is not the case.

I'll never forget the day one of my classmates wrote profanity on the blackboard. The entire class had to go before Mother Nazarene. She made us kiss the feet of Jesus (a statue of Jesus, that is) and swear that we did not write the forbidden words. Eventually a young classmate confessed that he wrote the words. Actually, he was innocent. And so was I, by the way, of that, anyway. Just in case you're wondering.

In high school I was quite a deceptive rebel. To those in authority over me, including my parents, I was the classic decent kid, but there was another side to the story. Nicknamed "Mark T. Brewer" (I liked "the brew"—get it?) by my friends, I was known to sometimes drink a quart of beer at lunch and then go back to class. I smoked pot, sold drugs to my friends, and did lots of other things that I am not now proud of throughout most of my high school and college years. These days I listen skeptically to those politicians and psychologists who think teenagers ought to be trusted to make good decisions in life and who argue that teens should be given more freedom from parental control. I believe teens need guidance and boundaries.

I can tell you from my experience that teens, especially teenage boys, need lots of monitoring and mentoring. Turning them loose and letting them make their own life decisions is a ticket to disaster. I thank God that, though I did plenty of things that could have turned out to be self-destructive, somehow the Almighty had his hand on my life for a greater cause. He was working in my life and I did not even know it. God uses a kind of spiritual stealth technology on us at times. We are often not even aware that he has us in his cross-hairs until, *bam*. Well, the *bam* was still a long ways off, but it would eventually get to me.

In high school I had a girlfriend whose name was Patty. I have no idea how the relationship lasted as long as it did. She was a sweet Italian girl and I was a rough construction-worker type. I was compulsively structured, neat and organized, and she was spontaneous and free spirited. Opposites attract, I guess, and we stayed together for three years.

Patty and Debbie were best friends. They even shared a room in Nana's and Pop-Pop's house near the hospital where they worked when they both did their student nursing assignments. When I would go over and hang out with Patty, Debbie was there, but I was intimidated by her. Remember—she was homecoming queen runner-up and all that, and I was, well, I was "Mark T. Brewer."

I recall the first time I ever saw her. I was stunned, thinking that she was as beautiful as the girls on the Lawrence Welk Show. (I guess I have just made myself out to be a relic of the ancient past with any young reader!) Like me, she was just a freshman, but she was standing near a phone booth with a tall, dark, and handsome junior. He was a varsity football jock. There I stood staring jealously at this gorgeous blond. Attempting to be inconspicuous, I felt small and insignificant. I knew she was in a different league from me.

The Beginnings of "Debbie and Mark"

Sometimes it seems that life throws you a bone when you are down and need it most. One night Patty dumped me. As she walked out of my life, she also informed me that Debbie liked me. I was deeply hurt that Patty had given me my walking papers-—after all, guys are supposed to break up with girls, not the other way around. But, wow, I was also filled with wonder and a sense of hope from the news about Debbie. If only it could be true! I knew it would be risky to invite her out on a date—even with the information from Patty. After all, how much faith can you have in the words of a girl who is in the process of cutting you loose? But I have always been willing to take my life into my hands in risk-taking (but that could be another chapter). So, anyway, I asked her out. The next night we had our first date—and wow, did we begin to fall in love!

I was head-over-heels in love with Debbie without mental reservation. And what really amazed me was that she felt the same way about me! She had all of the stuff that ought to have snagged her one of the "Most likely to succeed" titles. I could understand why I loved her; I just could not understand why she loved me in the same way. I could think of lots of reasons why she should not like me, but not very many about why she should. But I was not losing too much energy analyzing the situation. This was a breath of fresh air for me.

Debbie was shift manager at Friendly's Ice Cream while she was in college. Sometimes I would go there in the morning before the store opened and Debbie would cook up a special breakfast feast just for me. We got to start the morning with each other. When you can begin the day with the girl you are falling in love with, it gets the whole day off to a promising start. Anyone who has ever loved anyone understands that!

Pleasant days and months passed as I continued to attend college and she completed her nursing program. Then came the chance for her to work at a neurological clinic. There she worked directly with people who had multiple sclerosis. Many of these people had a progressive, unremitting, rapidly advancing type of the disease with irreversible physical deterioration. Her choice to work there is a story in itself. You see, she wanted for years to be a veterinarian. (Remember the pet rabbit and the petting zoo?) But a child's vision for her future often evolves with time, and one day Deb found herself eating chips and drinking soda while she sat on her bed and studied nursing. I think that deep inside what this meant was that she cared more for people than for animals.

Of course, becoming an RN is no easy thing, but she labored and worked and studied and then one day found herself in the position of head floor nurse at Chilton Memorial Hospital, working long hard hours and encountering many people with painful medical situations. With that responsibility comes the stress of making sure you are doing everything correctly—reading doctors' orders (not always an easy process) and making sure the doses are correct. It is work that is both important and, at times, tedious.

Though life began to fill itself more and more with many "to do" lists and with the complexities of existence that seem to attach to us like barnacles to the side of a ship, still Debbie always found ways of staying connected to those she loved and cared for. She might call you on the phone "just 'cause" and for no special reason. She'd bake brownies for her brother Glenn or for me. And, like the sweet chocolate aroma of fresh baked brownies, so her life was filled with the same kind of aroma of kindness for those she loved and held dear. She filled her days with love and laughter and with enjoying sunsets and the ice cream at Friendly's, and with feeding any stray animals that came across her path.

I remember one snowy morning we were together as she was heading for work. It was one of those magically romantic moments that all couples who have been together for a while can recall. It seemed life could never be better. We enjoyed everything about being together. Going out on dates, out to eat with friends, anticipating each new day—that was the norm for us. She liked Barry Manilow, especially his song, "Mandy," and I, well, I tolerated him! Small price to pay to be favored as this very special young lady's beau! You have to understand that I am just a regular guy on my best day. I am not a poet like Byron or Robert

Browning. I would never write words like, "My love is like a red, red rose that's newly sprung in June." I don't stand outside a girl's balcony romantically strumming a guitar and singing love ballads. But I loved my Debbie—and she loved me. And it was real, as real as anything like that can be.

But along with her love for me, I think she sometimes wondered, understandably so. I mean, I had this other side to my life. Frankly, I was a real deceiver. I had a tendency to be less than honest when it suited my purposes. I know she feared that there might be a deep, dark, downside to my character.

I didn't blame her. I knew that side was there. I was as yet unaware of the biblical teaching about human depravity. I had not, as far as I recall, read the verse in Jeremiah that says that the heart is deceitful above all things and desperately wicked (Jeremiah 17:9). But I knew I was not always transparent—that deep in my heart there was a side of me I was not entirely proud of. Yet I hoped Debbie would not really suffer the effect of the depths of that side of me, and I hoped she would love me in spite of myself.

She did. A few months after that first date we were engaged. I proposed to Debbie on Christmas, putting an engagement ring in her stocking. I knew even then she was the best thing that had ever happened to me. In spite of the fact that I was troubled within, I also knew that this was something real—perhaps the most real thing that had ever happened to me, and perhaps even my "last, best hope" for happiness in life. For me, she was the one. In fact, as far as I could see, she was the *only one*.

One winter day soon after we got engaged, we went out with some friends skating across a large reservoir …it was very secluded…middle of nowhere. She slipped and fell hard on the ice. I tenderly helped her up and told her she'd be fine. She tried to act as if the fall was nothing much at all. I had no idea that I'd be helping her up like that for the rest of our lives. It was probably best that I had no inkling at the time.

Just before we were married we had a special family dinner at my parent's home. Debbie was so nervous! In fact, she was crying. Debbie was very self-conscious. She had a difficult time being in front of a lot of people. Though I didn't know it at the time, it was a difficult moment for her in other ways, too. Later I learned she had been actually having second thoughts about marrying me. Could she really trust a guy like me? What about my old high-school reputation? What if I turned out to be a real jerk or if I would one day be unfaithful to her? Was my love real, or just an emotional attachment that might not survive the difficulties and challenges of life in the married world? I could understand her concerns—the truth was, I was not very deserving of her trust at the time.

Of course, neither one of us had any way of knowing just how those commitments would be tested in the months and years ahead.

Chapter 2

A Thing of Beauty

⁂

Our Wedding Day

AS THE HEAT of summer faded I breathed in that new, fresh autumn air. Coming soon was the day that the two *jars of clay* would in a new way, like never before, become melded together. Little did we know how our Master Potter had hand picked us to be *shaped* and *fired* together, in the way a skilled craftsman would shape and fire a beautiful clay jar. Then it arrived—October 13, 1979—the day I was to be united with my bride-to-be—my wife! I was twenty–two years old, and my mind was racing with anticipation about what lay ahead.

The church bells ringing, the crisp autumn air, the brilliant fall colors of the changing leaves—all of these sights and sounds brought glimpses of the change that would shape our lives. The fact that it was a fall wedding for us may also have been allegorical. As the daylight grows shorter and shorter in the autumn months, the leaves stop producing chlorophyll, and as a result, they change colors. What is actually happening is that as the green-colored fluid abandons the leaves, the true hues of the leaves become visible. We were marrying in what we thought was the springtime of our lives, but autumn would come quickly to our relationship due to the crisis we were about to face, and our true inner selves would be laid bare for us to see. Of course, we did not know that yet. As best as we knew, we had years of pleasant springs and summers ahead of us. Time would show us to be wrong about that.

My eyes searched for her, and there she was. Radiant blonde hair trimmed her breathtaking face. There was that sweet smile, her blue eyes hidden behind her lace veil. Everything was perfect. The words of the minister came, "In sickness and in health, for better or for worse." Those phrases echoed in the air, and like millions of brides and grooms before and afterward, we spoke them, almost as if by rote, I kissed my bride and left the church with the minister's pronouncement, "I now present to you Mr. Mark and Mrs. Debbie Grawehr." Our life began together as one.

Our wedding day was beautiful. Aren't they all? Well, probably not, but in the vast majority of cases, even with the kinds of problems that so often crop up during wedding ceremonies, in hindsight, wedding days are beautiful. Yet a wedding day, like other very important occasions, is filled with such significance and symbolism that there is always the potential for something to go wrong. Brides, especially, live in dread and fear of something going awry on their special day. Will there be a problem with the dress? Will the service go off without any significant problems? Will the family members all behave? Will the best man make an embarrassing speech?

Most of us have been to weddings that experienced some kind of mishap, whether minor or catastrophic, and no bride wants that to be her story. When such a thing happens, often it takes a lot of reflection before we can smile about it and recognize that it was a great day in spite of the difficulties. Well, our snafus were not catastrophic, but our special day did have its share of dark and frightening moments.

Imagine this with me, if you can. As we snuggled in the car on the way from the church to the reception, I noticed that something was wrong with Debbie. We had to pull the limousine over so she could vomit. Then again, you might have wanted to throw up as well if you had just married me!

But really, what was this all about? The question came to our minds, but we dismissed the thought, trying instead to savor the beauty of that picture-perfect day. Our reception was filled with food, fun, and the special warmth brought by family and friends. We were eager to fly away into the deep blue sky to our honeymoon getaway, Bermuda.

As I have reflected back to that autumn day, I remember that being in front of a lot of people always gave Debbie frets, and this was the supreme moment of stress. The wedding was *that* difficult for her. I am also sure that the combination of her doubts about whether she should marry me plus her natural fear of being the focus of attention was what produced that nervous stomach. These inner thoughts, these fears of "what if," this internal gnawing anxiety hiding behind the smiles and behind those beautiful eyes resurfaced again and again in the early weeks. But for the meantime we were able to set them aside.

The mind of a woman—that is a mystery I would only get a few glimpses of. How does a man understand the wonder, the beauty, the fears, the inner thoughts? Dark doubts lurked in the corners of my mind and sometimes peered around those corners, like sly foxes stalking their prey. How do you know whether you are making the right decision when you marry someone? Boy, if I could answer that question to everyone's satisfaction, I'd really be in demand on the lecture circuit! Match-making services move aside! I'd have the corner on the market.

The critical issues that are part of such a decision might not be clear to every twenty-two–year-old. After all, it is part of being young that you sometimes make decisions based more on emotions than reason. No one of course can be faulted for being young—it is simply part of the process that we are twenty before we are forty—but it certainly is the case that young people don't always know just what they want in life. Scientists even tell us that the brains of young people, especially young men, are not even fully formed physically until they reach about the age of twenty–one. (That may explain a lot!) So, young people often make bad choices when they marry, because like an intrepid first-time skier deciding to try the most difficult trail on the mountain, they are often unaware of the dangers lying before them on the path ahead.

But sometimes it *does* occur to them that they may be about to make the biggest mistake of their lives. Some especially conscientious young people recognize that this—supposedly the happiest day of their lives—could wind up being one of the most unfortunate.

Debbie was conscious of that. She was both happy and apprehensive at the same time. She was ready to plunge into the water, while at the same moment she was fearful that the water might turn out, after all was said and done, to be permanently cold. I admit, I was not the most trustworthy person at that time in my life. She had some sense of that. That was what made our wedding day such a mixed blessing to her. The book of Ecclesiastes says "to everything there is a season, a time to weep and a time to laugh." For Debbie, both of those times came on the same day and at the same hour—the hour when she said, "I do." The past tense of that is "I have done." Many a young bride or groom has soon after asked himself or herself, "Just what have I done?"

There would be no way for us ever to know for certain, but the anxiety of that day may well have been the trigger, the catalyst that sparked the disease, that caused that internal cracking to begin to occur. The future breaking of the precious jar of clay could have begun on that otherwise wonderful day. Her doctors would later suspect that, and so did I. Of course, in hindsight that makes our wedding day all the more a mixed blessing, especially for me. Unlike Debbie, I was really not plagued with doubts when I kissed her and made her my bride. But the possibility that the wedding itself may have initiated the downward spiral of her health that led to her death nearly seventeen years later certainly is a sobering thought. I must say that in the years ahead, I thought of the possibility often, and just as often felt a mixture of emotions.

Leaving behind the autumn colors of our wedding, we were eager to bask in the aquatic paradise off the coast of Bermuda, abandoning the cooling temperatures of New Jersey for a warmer climate where we could feel the warm sun on our faces. As we left on our honeymoon, she became sick on the flight out. Yet as everyone does, we hoped for the perfect honeymoon.

We arrived in Bermuda and once settled, enjoyed many fun-filled days and romantic nights, sipping Le Domaine Extra Dry Champagne from California. We breezed down small roads on our rented mopeds and had a blast. We shared passionate love and laughter, and I even remember running quite a distance only to flick sand from my bare feet as I breathlessly returned to my wife with a hot dog delivered to her beachfront cave. I enjoyed watching her face as she savored the mouthwatering flavor, at least as mouthwatering as a hot dog can be. Nearly everything we did in those days seemed as good as it could be.

We had wonderful moments together. We treasured those days, just the two of us. We saw skies bluer than any we could remember. The beach sand was sometimes cool, sometimes hot beneath our feet, even as the warm sea breezes filled the air with the salty tang of the Atlantic Ocean. Our evenings were special moments of quiet talk and romance. I felt that we were truly bonding together here on an island hundreds of miles from home. We held hands and smiled at each other in a paradise that was almost as unreal as the feeling that, for the first time in my life, I was no longer alone.

We were bonding in the way that only two people in that kind of relationship—marriage—can bond. For the moment, at least, we even dropped those fears that had plagued our thoughts in the days just before the wedding. We were as happy as any two people on a honeymoon could be. The only blight on our newlywed bliss was the fact that Debbie was still sick part of the time. In spite of that, though, she began to feel a little more confident that she had made a good decision in accompanying me to the wedding altar. I know that I was convinced that it was right from the very start. Our American dream had come true, despite the "blips in the curve," and our wonderful romance continued even after the honeymoon was over. In fact, it got better as the days went by.

When we returned home, I carried my new bride over the threshold. For a while, our life together was still a honeymoon. We had fun painting and decorating the old carriage house we had bought. Then there was the first time we had family members over for dinner. We were developing our own memories together, not merely being a part of someone else's. Our house overlooked a quaint little town, and we loved meeting the neighbors and looking at the town lights at night, listening to the Beatles and just enjoying our time together. Life was not exactly a Currier and Ives drawing, but we were really happy in those early days, and it only seemed at the time that it was going to get better.

Wonderful but Wobbly

Martin Luther, the famous Reformer who had previously been a Catholic monk, said that in the first year in the monastery, the Devil is silent. The first year of our marriage was good, but I can't say the Devil was completely silent. Both of us were stubborn. There were some stiff lumps in the clay, you might say. We began to discover very early that when two unique individuals become "one," that process can be difficult. I was a pretty typical guy of the 1970s, especially in my understanding of home interior decoration. I was very much into rock'n'roll music, and since I loved my stereo, I thought the ultimate in living room chic was to have speakers that served as end tables. What did I know? Just what is wrong after all with having Creedence Clearwater Revival blasting out from under your drink glass when you're tokin' on a joint with your friends around? Yeah, I was stereotypical of all of that culture from the late '70s, and some of it definitely was not very pretty.

As you might imagine, my tastes did not go well with Debbie. She, of course, wanted end tables bought from the furniture department, not the music department. Neither one of us was very good at communicating with each other, and in the heat of our disagreement over the decor, she stormed out of the house crying. I remember the sinking feeling I had as I watched her dash out to her blue Mustang, "Buggy," as she called it, and drove off in a flurry of frustration. I was angry also, but more angry with myself than with her. How can a marriage be *up* one moment and *down* the next? What causes that to happen? Can't a relationship, especially a marriage relationship, just work automatically? Why is it that feelings get in the way so often? As the saying goes, why can't we all just get along?

It would take me a while to learn really the best way to have a marital disagreement. In fact, I would not really learn how to do it well until another Person became part of our marriage relationship, but more of that later. In these early days of marriage I was simply discovering that a disagreement, even at a certain level what you might call a kind of verbal "fight," was going to be part of it. A husband was once asked whether he and his wife had any fights. He answered, "Oh yes, we fight real good." The grammar there might leave something to be desired, but I still had to learn the difference between "fighting good" and "fighting bad."

In those early days we had some parties at our house—big parties. We loved our music—Crosby, Stills and Nash, the Beatles, Barry Manilow. (I'll let you decide which ones were my favorites and which ones were hers.) People want to connect with others and to have a sense of being part of a group that is larger than themselves. It is a natural desire, one that is simply part of what it means to be human. The real question, of course is how do you fulfill that desire?

We had a lot of what we thought was fun in those days, but of course, we had yet to find the real source of joy we would eventually discover, or, I might say instead, that would one day discover us. Though our life was far from perfect, we had a relationship with each other that was real. It was a great starting point, and as I have said all along, I had no real doubts that it was right. *When you know, you know!* From day one I knew that she was the one for me, in spite of the complexity of the situation, and in spite of our own spiritual emptiness. Debbie was, simply, "my lady." There was no one else for me and, in spite of our immaturity and disagreements about things like home décor, we knew we had something special going.

We shared some wonderful times, like special snowy days. When the weather was really bad in the winter and I sometimes could not get to my job working construction, I would stay at home and we would enjoy very much being together. It was like a dreamland atmosphere—something from a Frank Sinatra song or an old black-and-white movie starring Bing Crosby or Fred Astaire and one of those blond actresses from the 1940s set in a Connecticut winter wonderland. Some people hate weather like that, but we grew to love it. This came to provide a kind of double contrast—the weather outside was frightful, as the song goes, but inside we were warm and delightful. Yet, though we did not know it then, we would realize later that the deeper level of contrast was the one between our developing tranquility and romance on the one hand and the nightmare that was about to come on the other hand.

For the time being, though, our life together seemed to get better with each passing day and week. People observing us from outside believed we had a great marriage, the American Dream being lived out in front of them. In many ways that was true, but as in most young marriages, that was not all of the truth. The darker side of my heart was yet to be exposed for who I really was, the core me that no one really saw, but that Debbie had occasional glimpses of. There was a vast and empty void in my life, one that I was trying to fill, but which seemed all the more empty with all my efforts.

We made the old carriage house really special together. That was one of my Dream Girl's dreams—to have a house with her special touch—and one of my dreams as well. We put our heart and soul into that house. It was very hard work, but the results brought us immense satisfaction.

It would not have occurred to me then that there was any parallel between our creative acts in that house and God's own creativity. As I remember those times now, I think of Adam in the Garden of Eden and how God told him to "subdue" the earth and bring it under his control. Adam had a big job before him, since he had little to work with except God's help and encouragement. (Though, come to think of it now, that is a pretty big advantage.) At least I had power tools, but it was still quite a job.

And yet, as if it was meant to be that way, I discovered great pride and happiness in taking raw and sometimes difficult materials and molding them into something both useful and beautiful. Eventually I would learn that God made us in his own image. Part of what that means is that we can take the same kind of joy in creating something or making something better than it used to be as God did in creation and still does in the re-creation of lives that need improvement. When we are building or making or creating something, in some sense at that moment we are like God.

There is, however, a problem. Adam rebelled against God in the Garden of Eden, and that act of rebellion brought sin and decay into what was otherwise a perfect world. That sin and decay are part of our heritage to this very day. Had there never been a fall into sin, every act of building or forming, from the simple fashioning of a small bird-house to the construction of a massive skyscraper, would have been at the same time an act of creation and obedience to and worship of God. It's also a way to imitate the Master Potter/Creator in our limited way as we use our hands to bring forth a recognizable object out of raw materials. Creating something new and improving upon something that needs improvement are tasks we are all called by God to perform; each to his own skills and according to his own abilities and interests, of course. Even in a fallen world that is no small thing.

A House Enlarged?

Debbie was everything I could have asked for in a wife. She loved to cook, sew, and keep the house clean. Keeping a neat house was important to me. The fact that she was committed to this task was part of the selfish reason I "loved" her. She wanted so much to please me and I appreciated it very much, probably more than I even told her at the time. She was even more thrilled with the prospect of being a mom. I was also interested in being a dad—at least theoretically. I talked about kids early on and how excited I would be when we had children. As things go, she became pregnant right after we were married. It was at this moment that reality came home to me—in spades.

Debbie had faced down the uncertainty of the future on our wedding day. As I have already made clear, I had no uncertainty about her being my bride. But as they say, what goes around comes around, and now it was my turn. Me? A dad? For real? Already? It was one thing to talk in generalities about being a father. Oh yeah, who doesn't want a piece of his own DNA running around the house, making him proud and carrying on the bloodline? Nearly every man in history has wanted that. It is just built into our genetic code. It is part of what makes men who they are, and it's also a part of their nature that sometimes causes men, and especially young men, to struggle to control their desires. Men typically have strong drives and this in some sense (even a divine sense, I now believe) is part of what will ensure the continuation of the human race.

So, it was not that I did not want to be a dad. I just did not want to be a dad at that very moment. Maybe in a couple of years I would be more ready for the responsibility. In Augustine's *Confessions* he relates a prayer he had prayed before he was saved: "Lord, make me chaste, but not yet!" If I had thought of praying a prayer at that time it would probably have been, "Lord, make me a dad, but not now!" In my selfishness I was seriously entertaining the idea of pursuing abortion. This really upset Debbie! I have a difficult time even fathoming that now, but that was where I was at that time.

As it turned out, being a dad at that time was just not going to be part of the story. Debbie miscarried in the early stages of the pregnancy. I was actually glad, though it brings me great pain to admit that now. She, of course, was deeply wounded, and I was not very sensitive to her feelings at the moment. All I could do was to breathe a sigh of relief. The contrast between us was huge—she wanted to be a mom; I was not ready for the task of being a dad. This is another indicator of the fact that, though we loved each other deeply, we were not yet on the same page. She had one set of priorities in our marriage and I had another set, maybe not completely different but still different. With the miscarriage it was clear that she would not become a mother at this time.

Furthermore, though she loved me, and though her dream for a wonderful marriage was on its way to being fulfilled, it would not be without some wrinkles. I had quite a temper, I admit. I was difficult to be around at times. Worse, I was arrogant toward her and sometimes treated her in a less than caring manner. I did as I wanted when I wanted, how I wanted. Living with Debbie was great, as long as she almost always did things my way. Often I was insensitive to her, to my own disgrace. She gave, and I took. That was pretty much the way of it at that time.

I was also still messing around with drugs and alcohol, so it often happened as I came down from my high that we would have a confrontation of some sort. When I would lash out at her, she would fight back. We both had our rough edges, but mine were more ragged than hers. Our marriage was wonderful in many ways, but like most marriages in the early stages, ours was pretty fragile. Wonderful but fragile. The problem is that the wonderful part was probably pretty superficial, but the fragile part went right down to the core. They say it is a miracle so many marriages survive the first year. I can identify with that miracle.

I would later discover that the Master Potter, being the incredible Designer he is, knew just the kind of circumstances that would break me and make me pliable in his hands. He knew what it was going to take for me to acknowledge him and create in me a desire to know and serve him. I filled my time with work, projects, my growing engineering and construction business. I was very busy, but in part I was simply attempting to fill the emptiness with things that were not capable of "fixing" my need. Little did I realize the worldly success that awaited me. Yet contrary to the way I was developing in my profession and career, I was not handling my personal life in a very responsible manner.

Winds of Change

During college my best friend was an atheist. Though I was raised Catholic, I became an agnostic during this time, as well. Though it may sound like a contradiction in terms, it is probably the case that there are quite a few Catholic agnostics, Baptist agnostics, and so on. I suspect this to be true at least on a practical level, since many people who claim to believe in God live their lives as though they are not really sure. But I was more than just a practical agnostic—I really was not sure whether there was a God at all.

I prided myself on being a hard-headed, clear-thinking man with a rational mind. In my way of understanding at the time, it was arrogant for a man to think he knows there is a God since God, if he is there, has not made that clear to us. Who could claim to know for certain? Where was the evidence for God's existence? Just what was the rational formula that made it unavoidable for thoughtful people to draw the conclusion that God truly *is?* Wasn't there just as much evidence *against* the notion that God is really there as there was in support of it? In fact, maybe there was more evidence against God than for him.

From the time I was in high school I loved construction and had a good idea of the direction that my vocational life would take. Ever since my Uncle Joe came by in his yellow air conditioning service truck, with the lift-gate and two way radio system, I knew where I was heading. Then my vocational school teacher encouraged me to go for an engineering degree. My father had always wanted me to go to college, but I rebelled and resisted because that was not what I wanted and because after all, it was my dad who was trying to encourage me to pursue a college degree. Yeah, I still had something of the rebel streak left in me. Still, I knew I loved designing and building things and that was the path my life would take.

My professional career took off even before graduating from Newark College of Engineering in 1979. In one of my night classes I met someone who knew of an upcoming employment opportunity, a perfect match for a guy like me. My first engineering job was at a pharmaceutical company called Hoffman–LaRoche. I could not have had a better job, working on designing and building a state of the art facility with the most sophisticated of building systems' infrastructure at the time. My boss was one of the most intriguing persons I had ever met, a Ukrainian with a rough background whose name was Oleh. Oleh knew his field as well as any man I had ever been associated with, and from the very first moment I began working with him I could not help but admire his skill and commitment to his job. But he also knew something else—something that would do more than help me put food on my table. He knew something that had the potential of changing my entire household. He knew Jesus Christ in a way I had never encountered before—on a personal level, as both a friend and a Savior.

Oleh talked to me about Jesus every chance he had—over coffee, in the car riding to the job, during work breaks. Even though I was an agnostic and proud of it, and did not want to listen to him, he was my boss and so I really had no choice. In my mind he was a fanatic. He would talk about the "rapture" of the church and the second coming of Christ and noted that at any moment he, Oleh, might just disappear.

I thought he was a *nut*. And yet, I also knew from working beside him, that he was, in reality, no mere religious lunatic. He was a "real man" with a real ability to work in and understand the issues of life and this world. And I also knew that he cared—cared deeply for the men who worked for him—that he cared deeply for me and for the well-being of both me and my wife. In other words, Oleh was an anomaly—a man of this world in his work skills and commitment to his job, and at the same time a man from another world when it came to his personal beliefs and moral convictions.

Oleh invited Debbie and me to a banquet, a meeting of the Full Gospel Business Men's Fellowship. We accepted his invitation, mostly out of a sense of obligation to him as my boss. But I was not immediately drawn into the fold. In fact, I was very uncomfortable at that meeting. The people who spoke that evening talked about faith, Jesus Christ, and walking with God in your business life. Their language was like a foreign tongue to me. I didn't know what I was doing there except that my friend and boss had invited me and it seemed the polite thing to do to accept. But I was miserable.

I remember rolling my eyes, making eye contact with one of the waiters who knew I was not *into* all of this stuff. He wasn't either, but gave me the glance that says, "Hey, buddy, I am here for the tips, so I can smile at their jokes, but have my real laughs later when I think of how silly these people are." As I remember my attitude then, I realize that to an outsider, the Christian faith sometimes seems less than practical and more than a little bit unnatural. In some sense, of course, all of that is true. There are mysteries right at the heart of the Christian message, mysteries such as the Trinity. But in another sense the Christian faith is the most practical and believable set of ideas and relationships that one could ever imagine. I just did not know that at the time.

Debbie felt the same way as I did. This was not our element and never had been. We were *normal people*, or at least that is how we viewed ourselves, and normal people just don't get excited about heaven and Jesus and the Bible. Normal people are concerned with building houses, making a living, raising a family, and retiring with a nice nest egg. I could not understand why Oleh was so taken by all of this Christian stuff. I saw it as a crutch—a crutch for people who are too weak to face the issues of life without some kind of fairy tale to hold them up. I certainly did not believe that Jesus was God, and that was really what this was all about, was it not?

Not long after the banquet, the trial would begin. We would have to face the challenge of dealing with the disease that would later kill my Dream Girl. Our lives were about to undergo a drastic change. Actually, we were about to experience a series of changes, and rapid ones at that. We were in no way prepared for the storm we were about to face. But then, "normal people" have a severe handicap when it comes to facing a challenge that is anything *but* normal.

Chapter 3

God's Handiwork with Fragile Vessels

~《《○

Prelude to a Trial

DEBBIE AND I were married and began living out our dream together in our new home. We were fast on our way to becoming the quintessential American couple. But that was not to be our story. A hint of the nightmare to come emerged one day when I went out for a run. Debbie came with me and was jogging along behind, when from the corner of my eye I suddenly saw her stumble and nearly fall over. I realized she was really struggling. I had to hold her arm so she could walk upright. It was a kind of scary moment, yet it passed, and we had no idea at that moment that it was just the beginning of worse things to come.

Debbie immersed herself in her job in our local hospital. Previously, she had interned at Welkind Neurological Hospital, a facility dedicated to the care of people with multiple sclerosis. It was there that she was trained to work with people who had MS. She took care of patients who were among the worst cases. She had one severely afflicted patient whose nickname was "Itch," probably because itching is one of the manifestations of MS. It shook Debbie to the core of her being to see people in such a terrible condition. She shared with both me and her mother on several occasions the deep fear she had of this disease. It almost seemed as if she had a premonition that she was preparing in her nurse's training to face the dark shadow that lay over our future. I did not pay much attention to that at the time, though.

Debbie began working as a registered nurse. Because of her ever-present strong work ethic, she always found herself at the front of the pack among her coworkers. Always early to work and late to leave, she was promoted quickly. But as you might imagine, there was a lot of pressure with her job. Dealing with the medical condition of horribly ill people brings a giant strain into one's work environment. You have to decipher doctor's orders that are often, as the cliché goes, scribbled almost indecipherably. You have to be sure the medication you give is exactly right, precisely the correct dosage. You do this over and over again for many patients all day, every day. You know that a single mishap could cost a patient his or her life. It is not merely a case of causing someone discomfort by a mistake, because mistakes could mean fatalities. The thought of it can worm its way into your consciousness so much that all you can think about is the fear of doing something wrong. Most of the time Debbie dealt pretty well with that, but it was always there as a lingering fear that she had to often suppress.

After a while, Debbie began to notice that the fluorescent lights in the hospital were bothering her. They made her nauseous and also seemed to affect her in various neurological ways. (We later learned one of the neurological effects is called *nystagmus*—the eyeball begins to jitter uncontrollably.) Then she began to have problems with balance. She felt dizzy much of the time, as she had the day we went jogging. She began to be very afraid; she knew something was wrong, and she was fearful of finding out just what it might be—we both were. Some people refuse to go to the doctor because they are afraid of what he or she might tell them. Debbie was not like that at all, yet I think she understood that anxiety over just what the doctor might say when he looked at her over the top of his glasses. And so, not very long after we had experienced the bliss of being newlyweds, a tsunami of a trial began to wash over us.

The Diagnosis

Having cared for many others with MS and knowing well the symptoms of it,* Debbie tentatively diagnosed herself with multiple sclerosis in early 1980. Then the doctors confirmed her fears. We heard the devastating news via a phone call from the neurologist. As he got me on the phone, he simply told me, without much of an introduction, the bad news in quite a matter-of-fact way. Debbie had MS. What this really meant was yet to be seen, but it already didn't sound good at all. What we did not realize was that she had the rare and most aggressive kind of this disease. Not knowing what would be ahead, the fear of the unknown held my feelings in its cold grip. As Debbie watched my reaction, he asked me not to tell her. Imagine! I guess this was the first of many tests to come, and perhaps I failed this one. I was ticked off at the doctor, and at God—the God I wasn't even sure I believed in—as well.

First of all, the doctor. While I might not have been the most compassionate guy around, for sure, I still couldn't believe the crass gall of this professional wing nut! He was telling me my life as I had known it might just be over, and he was telling it to me with all of the compassion of someone reporting the next week's weather forecast. And then to tell me that I ought to keep this awful information from my dear wife, whose life it would most impact! Time just seemed to move in slow motion as I listened to his words and Debbie watched me. It was almost as if I didn't have to tell her what the doctor was communicating to me. She seemed to already know. But I didn't want to tell her! I simply didn't want to believe it. No, I didn't believe it!

---

* Let me offer try to explain a little about MS: It is a disease of the central nervous system in which the body's defense system attacks myelin, the fatty substance that surrounds and protects the nerve fibers in the central nervous system. It sometimes also attacks the nerve fibers themselves. The damaged *myelin* forms scar tissue, a process called *sclerosis*. Nerve impulses traveling to and from the brain and spinal cord are interrupted, producing a variety of symptoms affecting some or many parts of the body including gait and movement (which can lead to paralysis), speech, vision, hearing, bladder and bowels, swallowing, and even respiration. Many MS suffers have what is commonly called "relapsing-remitting" MS—they go into remission from time to time. A minority get a variety of MS that "progresses" (a terrible word but accurate) into a more and more severe form of the disease. That's what Debbie had.

Secondly, God. Just who is he, anyway? Oleh talked about him being an all-powerful, all loving God. Would a God of love have allowed this to happen to the woman of my dreams? And if he is love, then why is this happening to us? If this all-powerful God was truly a God of love then surely he would want to do something about Debbie's condition. I did not know just what that might be, but surely it would be something. Perhaps the doctors would be able to say to me, "We have somehow made amazing breakthroughs in treating this illness." Maybe those innovations would have come from this loving God. Or, why could he not just heal my wife? I did not know the Bible very well, but I knew that such things happened in the Bible.

Or perhaps Oleh was correct that God is love, but perhaps he has no power over things like multiple sclerosis, I would reason with myself. He would like to fix people's problems, but these things are just outside his ability to effect. If this were the case, God would be a very compassionate being, but just incapable of helping people out of some difficulties. But if that is the case, then what does it mean to say that he is God? I thought the definition of God was that he could do whatever he wished. Certainly that was what Oleh was saying. God is both all-powerful and all-loving, in Oleh's opinion. But now I faced a potentially devastating situation in my own life that might just show that God, if God existed at all, could not be both of these at once.

Many things went through our minds in a flash. Where did the illness come from? When did it begin? Could it have been prevented? We recalled that one time, when we were ice skating, when Debbie had fallen and hit her head. Did that fall play a role? Was the stress of our wedding day the spark that set it off? Was it the stress of her job? We agonized over the question of what had brought this on. If it was not some natural result of a fall or stress, was it something else? We were told it was not contagious, but that was sure difficult for us to rule out. The spring of 1980 was the first time we asked those kinds of questions. It would not be the last time.

One thing was suddenly and stunningly real. Our dream had turned to a nightmare. The type of MS that struck my wife was eerily subtle at first, though that would quickly change. We almost immediately fell into a pattern of hope and let-down, hope and let-down. Nearly half a million Americans acknowledge having this disease, but neurologists believe the real number is twice that amount. One of the reasons for this discrepancy is that many people have MS and do not know it. In their cases the symptoms are not profound. They may have a nervous tick or struggle with fatigue; they may have a loss of muscle coordination or experience vision problems or slurred speech. They write it off to normal factors—they work too hard, they are just getting older, a member of their family had something similar happen to him or her and it was really not a serious problem. Often those who have the disease do not suspect that they have been stricken by one of the most terrifying diseases known to man. And unless their symptoms become much worse, in many cases they see no reason to seek a medical diagnosis for their difficulty.

Learning to Cope with the Onslaught

Debbie and I had no such good fortune. The disease moved like a Class IV hurricane through her system. Day by grueling day her body became a veritable death house, stealing precious life away from her in the way the lapping of the ocean erodes a sand bar, wave by wave. It was as if her life was going to be an example of seventeenth-century philosopher Thomas Hobbes's observation that for most people, life is "nasty, brutish, and short." The brute force of her ailment was becoming obvious and we were already confronted with the prospect that her years would probably be miserable and few, or, maybe even worse miserable and *many*. Either prospect was terrifying—especially, of course, for her.

Even with the quick development of symptoms that we witnessed in the early weeks after the diagnosis, we had no way to prepare ourselves for the incredible speed with which the plague of MS ripped through Debbie's bodily systems. Her vision was one of the first things affected as her sight became blurred, and then increasingly she had a difficult time focusing. She was extremely sensitive to heat. Her voice became compromised with tremors. Her motor skills were being lost at a dizzying speed. We hoped against hope that the progress of the disease would lessen and that she would level out and stabilize at some point. But that was not to be the case. Each time another exacerbation set her back we hoped she would revert to her former condition or that she would at least remain stable and in remission. The opposite would actually turn out to be the case.

We have all had to consider worst-case scenarios, but in most of those situations, fortunately, the "worst case" is not what eventually happens. In our situation, the worst case *was* the case. It could hardly have been any more agonizing. My wife was rapidly losing her vision and becoming paralyzed from her neck down. Her speech was growing more and more inarticulate. A year after the diagnosis I could still understand her, but few others could; within two years she had lost all powers of anything resembling real speech and had become legally blind. At this time she began to communicate with us by writing on a tablet, while she still had possession of some motor functions in her arms and hands.

The woman I married, in the prime of health and with great expecta-tions for the future, was trapped in a functionless body at twenty-three years of age. One of the last comments she would offer prior to losing her voice completely, was the phrase "small potatoes." Whenever people would complain about some problem or other, Debbie would say they had "small potatoes." She was saying, in so many words, "If they really want to understand the real basis for complaining about the unfairness or injustice of what life throws at you, they should spend a couple of days wearing my slippers."

Debbie had a Siamese cat. This cat had an attitude (don't they all?). The cat would always stay on her lap, and often it sat on her in a way that was uncomfortable to Debbie. "She wants what she wants when she wants it," Debbie would say. What a luxury to have what you want when you want it! When your body is afflicted with a disease like MS, you give up such a luxury, and many others beside.

We have probably all heard the adage, "I complained that I had no shoes until I saw a man who had no feet." In those early days of Debbie's illness I would be around people at work or at the grocery store, or maybe just walking from one place to another in the course of the day. I would overhear their conversations about their problems. You know the kinds of conversations I am talking about—they are replayed over and over again in every American city every day. A woman does not like the fact that her husband works late hours. A man complains that his boss has unrealistic expectations, and he hates it. Another person is upset because his doctor can't seem to prescribe the right decongestant to help with his allergies and he has to carry facial tissues in his pocket all the time.

I don't mean to disparage the everyday hassles and nagging problems that people have. I know those things can build up in a person's life and become significant issues to the one experiencing them. But I have to say that as I listened to people talk about the challenges of everyday life, I often wanted to interrupt their conversations and say to them, "Count your blessings, Pal. Do you want to know what it is like to deal with a real problem?" Small potatoes, indeed!

We all need a sense of perspective. Someone under a sentence of death once said, "The knowledge that you are going to die tomorrow tends to focus the mind wonderfully." I imagine so! Living with a spouse who is profoundly ill and who is falling to pieces physically before your very eyes day after day also helps one understand the difference between a real problem and a "bad hair day." In many ways I am thankful for the fact that I had begun to learn that lesson, though I might have preferred to learn it another way. The difference between the two has been forever branded into my consciousness.

Learning to Live a Dying Life

Over the first year or so, Debbie and I both went through tremendous frustrations. We were both angry. She felt the dual strain of having this terrible ailment along with the recognition that she had become a burden on me. I was no longer simply bread winner; I was also cook, nurse, and housekeeper—and she hated the fact that I was forced to carry such a load. Her dream of being the wife that I wanted her to be was dying fast and instead becoming a weight of guilt she carried around with her. I was working all day long at a very demanding job, and then at the end of the day I had my responsibilities toward Debbie. Family helped out a great deal, but they had their lives and complications to take care of as well.

The fact is that I had neither the energy, the patience, nor the desire to be nurse to my wife. Every day there were meals and the housekeeping. Debbie had always kept a very neat house, but now that job was in the hands of someone who had little time for such things. That in itself was also a source of frustration for her. In a short time, Debbie needed some help in dressing, and eventually she needed to be dressed completely by someone else. Medicines had to be administered. Bathroom basics were eventually carried out in a way similar to caring for an untrained baby. No one liked that, especially not Debbie, but there was no option. Daily she had to have her back strategically and very firmly patted (*percussing* they called it) in order to keep her lungs clear. As someone once said, the only problem with life is that it is so *daily*. Ours was definitely a life that was daily. It was essentially a hopeless sentence of death, though we did not yet know that the illness would be terminal.

We did begin to hire help, especially in the form of home health aides. That had its own set of complications, which I will discuss in some detail later on. As I said, the disease and its unrelenting challenges was an incredible burden placed on a young couple—a young couple who at this time in their lives had not yet discovered the Ultimate Resource that would enable them not only to endure, but also to conquer this giant threat. But we had to face it. Debbie began to find a way to cope earlier than I did, and over time she developed the kindest heart and most winsome spirit imaginable. That, however, was still in the future from our vantage point in late 1980.

My "coping" was a different story. My thought was, "What is up with this?" My life had been ruined. How could God do this to me? Conventional medicine didn't seem to be doing anything. Over the next few years we would try remedies that we heard about via the MS sufferers' grapevine. Yet each time we tried an experimental drug it seemed that the side effects were worse than any relief it might bring. We spent long, long nights together at Rockefeller University Hospital in New York City. We tried everything—vitamins, doctors, healing services, medications. We flew to an off-the-wall clinic in Tijuana, Mexico to seek alternative intervention. We sought out different kinds of doctors, nutritionists, and whole food and herbal remedies. We tried acupuncture, chelation and even goat cell therapy. One woman even tried to convince us to have Debbie drink her own urine daily! (That one we skipped.) We were hoping that at the very least we could simply find a way to slow the progress of the disease.

I searched for every possible resource to deal with this enemy, hoping at the very least to find something that would retard the process of its development. Nothing worked. In fact, it seemed almost as though everything we tried just made matters worse. I am sure now that this was not the case, but it certainly seemed that way at the time. By the five year mark since the diagnosis I was at my wits' end, and my inability to solve this problem myself was a new experience to me. As a tradesman I was skilled at fixing or rebuilding broken things. As an engineer I was trained to solve difficult problems and create solutions. I was good at attacking a project and, by making it subject to my ingenuity and hard work, forcing it to turn out the way I wanted. But with Debbie's illness, this fix-it man was completely helpless.

Debbie's doctor asked her to begin journaling her illness in order that we might be able to correlate what it is that could possibly be working at all. In the early stages when she could use her hands, she would write down every detail she could think of—especially her physical, emotional, and mental (*PEM*, in medical parlance) states throughout the day. We also kept a very close watch on her diet. She would record her emotional condition at various times of the day—when she was hopeful and happy, when she was in depression and even in despair. On at least one occasion she wrote that she wanted to die. Other times her emotions ran the gamut from apathy to aggravation, disgust, and anxiety. She once wrote in her PEM journal that she saw best in dim light, but that even then it ached to try to focus. Soon that would no longer be an issue.

Let me diverge for a moment to ask you to think of what it would be like to be trapped in a body becoming more helpless almost by the day. The path was the reverse of the one children take as they grow. If you have small children in your extended family and you only get to see them three or four times a month, it seems like they have changed every time you see them. But theirs is a change of growth and upward development; Debbie's was a change of decline, decay and a spiraling down into a hell of helplessness. People who only saw her a couple of times a month saw the ongoing ravages of change—a change that was obvious, tragic, and unstoppable.

I finally had to face the fact that we would not have the things we hoped to have. All my dreams appeared to have been shattered by this awful illness. My emotions mirrored Debbie's in many ways, though I think my down moments in some ways were worse than hers. (Isn't it curious that I was so concerned with "my dreams," "my emotions," "my down moments"? Could it be I was more than a little self-involved at the time?) My feelings skyrocketed up, and then plunged down to the very depths. Even worse than that was the numbness that would assail me between my ups and downs, even though at times I wished I could be numb. I remember the rock group Pink Floyd's famous album, *The Wall*. At the high point (or low point) of the whole story as told in that album, the man narrating the account says that he finally became "Comfortably Numb," which, incidentally, is the title of a song on the album.

I want to affirm from experience that there is nothing comfortable about being numb. Instead that numbness reminds you that you may never again have a moment of normalcy. From the diagnosis on, we would never again be a "normal" family. There would be no Sunday afternoon bicycle rides for my wife and me. There would be no strolls through the park and off to ice cream afterwards. There would be no pitter-patter of little feet in the mornings—children waking up and running in to get Mommy and Daddy out of bed to fix them breakfast. There was only one extra occupant of our house—the Disease—and that guest would take up residence and become a fixture of our life together. Or so it seemed at the time. Surely, this was not helping me to believe in a loving and Holy God.

When I thought of our struggle, it often seemed like a veritable Mount Everest of intimidation rising up before me. Who could face such a challenge? I was certainly no emotional athlete, the kind of person who could face any kind of problem with calmness and fortitude. I was just a typical engineer with enough of my own personal issues already in my life. This was the kind of difficulty that could only be faced by some great person of enormous personal courage. That was not a description of me in any sense of the word, or so it seemed to me at the time. We were confronted by a problem that was far bigger than we were. It was only when we came to recognize that fact that we were eventually enabled to find a way to make something of it.

Chapter 4

Trying to Cope
Without Knowing How

~✠◎

Another Full-Time Job

PEOPLE HAVE SKILLS and gifts that are conveyed to them through both genetics and experience. Some folks are natural scholars and thinkers; others are great at working with people; still others are adept at working with numbers and calculations.

I was a designer-builder. I loved my work and I loved everything associated with it. I enjoyed conceiving a project, planning out what it would take to make it a reality, and then the work involved in seeing it through to completion. I enjoyed looking at the final product and taking joy in knowing that I had been there from the first pencil drawing to the last nail, weld, or screw. I loved it and both by nature and training was made for that kind of work. I still do love it—it is always a joy to work at such tasks.

I have a difficult time identifying with people who can't decide what they want to be when they grow up. Thankfully, for me this was not a struggle at all. Finding your vocational calling in life is not very difficult—just find out what you love to do and then figure out a way to make a living at it. As long as your goals are noble and you live with integrity toward others, there is almost always a way to make your love into your living, though it may take a lot of both inspiration and perspiration for it to happen. I knew my calling at that time, and it was building stuff.

My calling was certainly not nursing! Yet, due to the circumstances of our life together, there I was, through no choice of my own, serving as a nurse to Debbie. I was bi-vocational, you might say, a designer-builder on the day shift and a private nurse on swing and graveyard shifts. Debbie had a character that was well-suited for nursing; as far as I knew, I was not so well-suited. That was probably part of the old "opposites attract" cliché at work that we are all so familiar with. One of the things that had drawn me to her was that she had the kind of heart and talents that made her a good nurse, skills and passions that I did not have—but which I knew were beautiful and wholesome and admirable. She did it by nature.

Now I had to be something that I was not naturally suited to be. I had to learn skills I had never known, but it was more than that. For me to become part-time nurse to Debbie I had to be someone I had never had to be before, at least not in that way. My "day job" witnessed me conceiving new designs, performing sophisticated calculations, giving instructions to subordinates, checking on the progress of work being done, affirming some workers and critiquing others. Second shift had me preparing and serving food and then washing dishes. I administered medicine, made beds, washed linens and other clothing, gave baths and undressed and redressed my increasingly disabled wife. I don't think I would have been a very good nurse to just anyone, but this was not *just anyone*, and I slowly and reluctantly learned how to give the kind of care she needed. Looking back, quite frankly, I think my contribution was pretty superficial. Down deep, I was actually growing bitter over what I was being required by circumstances to do.

In addition, I was not doing my nursing work as a profession. Most hospital nursing jobs have schedules that run three or four days a week. One of the psychological reasons for this is that nursing drains a person. Professional nurses need longer recovery time from their work than does, say, a carpenter. There is that stress that goes along with nursing, having to get things right all the time. But there is also another kind of stress—the sheer intensity of being with patients, some of whom have terrible illnesses and some of whom are dying.

The challenge for a nurse is even greater when the patients know that they are slowly dying. Taking care of dying people for a living gives one an entirely different outlook on life than most people have whose professions do not require them to walk into rooms every day where people have just been given a "number" by their physician—"Six months, perhaps a little longer." We have all been around people who have been given such news, but most of us don't work with them every day. That very experience often requires that ER nurses, critical care nurses, and ICU nurses work only those three-day schedules or something similar. They need those extra days off to prepare for the next round. And they are caring for permanently ill people who are not even personally close to them. Sure I had help here and there, but that was mostly when I was gone. I was basically a seven-day-a-week nurse who could not ignore the need; I had one patient, and that patient was the largest part of my own personal world.

The point I am making is that at times we all have to become something we are not. We all play to our strengths, but often life does not allow us simply to do the things we do best or enjoy most. Men and women alike have to step forward and take on tasks that have to be done though they themselves may not be well-prepared or best constructed to do those things. In my opinion, the phrase, "That's not my job" ought not to be in anyone's vocabulary, whether at work, or simply in regard to life in general. Michelangelo might have refused to paint the ceiling of the Sistine Chapel, because, after all, he was not a painter but a sculptor. Pope Julius insisted, however, and Michelangelo did the work, though it required him to lie on his back on a scaffold for eighteen months. Add to that the fact that Michelangelo had a bad back. He went through a great deal of pain and difficulty to take on a task that was not his strength in order to accomplish a noble goal. (By the way, Michelangelo, not a bad job for the first time out!) In my case there was no artistic ability needed (thankfully!). Rather, a *designer and builder* became *amateur nurse* because he had to do so for his wife and to deal with what life brought him. But nursing a young lover who is suffering in the prime of her life and not being able to predict how much worse it might get seemed so contrary to the way I thought things should be.

That nurse was becoming more and more filled with anger, anger at the circumstances, anger at God, and anger at the world in general.

The Hound of Heaven

While I was playing the role of nurse—nurturing my growing bitterness along with caring for Debbie–God was playing the role of Seeker. We hear a lot these days about seeker-sensitive and seeker-driven congregations. I am sure that it is very important for churches to be able and ready to reach people who are looking for answers in life. That is all well and good. What church strategists and theologians sometimes forget is that the seeking begins, not with people looking for answers and not with churches laboring to accommodate such persons, but with God himself. God is the greatest Seeker of all, as Scripture so clearly testifies, and he had now set about to bring both Debbie and me to the truth.

Of course, he did not merely begin that task when Debbie got sick. In fact, God had been working and planning to bring the two of us to the place of spiritual healing even before the creation of the physical world—"He chose us in him before the creation of the world," the apostle Paul writes in Ephesians 1:3-5. When our minds become awakened to the fact that God is calling us to himself, we often form the belief that we are the ones moving toward him. "I finally found God," says someone who has just trusted Christ for salvation. That is certainly not wrong, for no one experiences God's redemptive work without repentance and faith. But it is even more true to say that God finds us. As the Scripture says about a woman named Lydia in the book of Acts, "The Lord opened her heart to respond to the things spoken by Paul" (Acts 16:14).

Francis Thompson, an English poet who died in 1907, penned the work *The Hound of Heaven*, in which he imagines God as a hound pursuing those being saved until they are finally exhausted of fleeing. These lines from that work speak volumes:

> Fear wist not to evade as Love wist to pursue.
> Still with unhurrying chase,
> And unperturbéd pace,
> Deliberate speed, majestic instancy,

Came on the following Feet,
And a Voice above their beat—
"Naught shelters thee, who wilt not shelter Me."

"Naught shelters thee, who wilt not shelter Me." Well, I was not yet ready to shelter God in my heart, but in the months following Debbie's diagnosis, it would become increasingly clear that nothing would shelter me from God's relentless call. I wanted nothing to do with religion, even more so now that my life had been shattered. But God was placing all kinds of things directly in my path, even as he stalked me from behind.

My boss was a Christian, as I have already mentioned. He was persistent, that's for sure, but not obnoxious. He never browbeat me. He simply represented Christ faithfully to an employee whose life was filled with a very unusual challenge. I believe he was confident I would come to the knowledge of the truth. His confidence did not rest in anything he saw in me, and certainly not even in his own ability as a Christian witness. He was confident that the God to whom he had entrusted his life would be effective in seeking and winning us to himself. In all of this, God was opening my heart to respond to spiritual truth and causing me to see spiritual truth in a way I had never seen it before. As once the scales fell from the apostle Paul's eyes when he finally understood the gospel message (Acts 9:18), so something similar was happening with Debbie and me.

At this time I also began to read books by Christian authors. I was not ready for anything too heavy—I had enough intensity just in dealing with the rapid deterioration and increasing needs of Debbie. Had someone handed me any books that were too theological or that used exclusively "Christian language," I would have had a much harder time coming face to face with truth. I love many of those books now, but I would not have been able to handle them at that time. What I needed was hope and encouragement, and I found them through a variety of books.

This is important. Christians have to find a way to speak to their generation and to its subgroups in language that the groups understand, without diluting the Christian message. I found language that spoke to me in my vernacular in a free book, oddly enough, on the checkout counter in a hardware store, a book entitled *An Engineer Evaluates the Bible.* You could not get any more into my language than that! There is some kind of irony in the fact that I, as a builder, was helped in finding my way to Christ by visiting a hardware store. Maybe "Ace is (was) the place!"

That fortunate experience would have been similar to a building tradesman coming to Jesus as a fellow tradesman. This book really helped me realize the likelihood of the authenticity of the Scriptures. It made its case by simply developing the mathematical probability that the fulfillment of the prophecies could not have been by accident. It was fascinating for me to read a book in which the author used probabilities in mathematics to establish the reliability of the Bible through the fulfillment of the prophecies. Mathematics! That was my turf! I was a scientific-type guy, a man of the world, not a religious person.

I also could no longer accept the claim by purely naturalistic scientists that everything we see in the world around us is merely the product of nature plus time plus chance. The notion that all living things have their origins in some primordial slime pit and that it all happened merely by natural selection made no sense to me. The odds are simply against that happening. I became convinced that God must exist.

As I noted earlier however, I still had intellectual difficulties with Christianity. I just could not believe that Jesus was God, and without that, you can't be a genuine, biblical Christian. Christians are not just people who go to church; they are people who affirm that Christ was who and what he claimed to be, and who follow his "call" to be the kinds of disciples he wants them to be. About this same time I also discovered the writings of Josh McDowell. If you have ever read his apologetic arguments, you would know that he could be very helpful at this point. There are more sophisticated thinkers than McDowell out there defending the Christian tradition, but again, I did not really need sophistication. Not at that point. I needed someone who could communicate on a level that was accessible and made sense to me, a practical man dealing with the challenges of life and looking for meaning and significance in my struggles.

McDowell argued that Jesus was either a liar, was insane, or else he was the very Son of God as he claimed to be. Many have tried to make the case that Jesus was a respected prophet and teacher in first-century Palestine, but that he was only a prophet and teacher and not the unique Son of God in the flesh. But the argument simply does not work, and I came to see the holes in the reasoning through McDowell's help and guidance. Jesus asserted, for instance, that no one could know God unless he (Jesus) revealed God to that person (Matthew 11:28-30). Jesus also claimed that before even Abraham existed, that he (Jesus) existed (John 8:58). At the end of the gospel of John, Thomas called Jesus, "My Lord and my God" (John 20:28). Jesus responded by saying, "You have seen and believed. More blessed are those who, having not seen me, yet believe." In the seventh chapter of John, Jesus stated that if anyone believed in him, out of his being would flow rivers of living water. These are the kinds of things that God says about Himself in the Old Testament. In addition, Jesus is actually called "God" several times in the New Testament (e.g., John 1:1; Acts 20:28). The evidence that Jesus saw himself to be the Son of God, God incarnate (God in the flesh) is overwhelming in the New Testament.

But the capstone to the argument is the resurrection of Jesus from the dead. McDowell helped me see that there is no plausible explanation for the story of the empty tomb in Jerusalem except the explanation that is given by the gospel writers. Jesus actually rose from the dead, never to die again. As many scholars are quick to point out, the alternative explanations just don't work. Jesus did not simply "swoon" on the cross and then revive in the tomb. A crucified man would not have been able to roll the stone away and scare off the Roman guard. The disciples did not go to the wrong tomb. Had they done so, the Jewish and Roman leaders could simply have produced the real body. Jesus did not survive the crucifixion and disappear into the mists of history with Mary Magdalene, as claimed by Dan Brown's book, *The Da Vinci Code*. There is no evidence for that, in spite of all of the sensational noise caused by that book.

One recent critic has thrown up his hands and confessed that none of the alternative explanations for the resurrection make sense, but since we know that dead men don't rise, it must be that dogs ate the body of

Jesus off of the cross. That is his explanation for the absence of a corpse. In his view there could not have been a resurrection, but the alternatives offered over the centuries simply are not plausible, so we are left with whatever we can fabricate.

There is something seriously wrong with these arguments. One of the things wrong with them is that they contend, "Well, we know there can't have been a real resurrection, so we have to find some other solution to explain the empty tomb." In other words, they begin with a presupposition (that resurrection is not possible) and then argue to find support for that presupposition. That is circular reasoning by any accepted definition.

I became convinced that McDowell was correct. Either Jesus was a liar, or he was insane, or he was telling the truth. But it is clear that Christ was not a liar, since he was the most righteous of all persons who ever lived and since he developed a moral ethic in his teachings that is unparalleled. It is also clear that Jesus was not insane. His teachings are among the most logical and lucid teachings in all of human history. He predicted his own resurrection, and he was right. No insane person could have done that. So, it must be that Jesus was who he said he was, and who the other New Testament writers said he was, God wrapped in human flesh.

Over a period of weeks of contemplation and study, I became *intellectually* convinced that Christianity was true. In a sense I had come to the point at which Augustine arrived in the fifth century. He became intellectually certain of the truth of the faith by his own study and by listening to Bishop Ambrose preach. But his heart still had not been changed. He still needed to be "born from above." Whether I yet knew it or not my need was indeed similarly desperate.

In addition to the intellectual issues, I needed someone to help me to deal with practical objections as well as the philosophical ones. Many people, like me at the time, don't look for an iron-clad argument for the truth of the faith, but rather they look to see if Christians are willing to walk the talk and not just offer up lip service to the faith. Does the Christian faith address those matters that are part of the reality of existence, such as life and death, financial distress and poverty, pain and suffering? More than that, does the Christian faith deal with these matters in a straightforward and honest manner? Are Christians trying to do something about all the suffering in the world? I did not need a sophisticated chain of logic, but I needed it to be *right*, and I needed it to be *real*. If I was going to give consideration to this faith, I needed to have a sense that it was not just wishful thinking.

Not long after the nineteen-year-old Charles Spurgeon began his famous ministry in London in 1854, a church member invited the well-respected theologian Robertson Nicoll to come hear the young pastor preach. When Nicoll left that day, he commented, "I have never heard anything that *real* in my life." I wanted that same reality, nothing less. McDowell helped me understand that my objections to the Christian faith were not very profound, and that the real evidence points to the fact that Jesus really was (and is) who he said he was and who Christians claim he is. My intellectual acceptance was accomplished, but it takes more than merely a convinced mind to make one a believer. Still, it was a move in the right direction.

And as my mind became convinced of the truth of Jesus' claims, I also became more and more interested in what Christian leaders were saying. As I dialed through the radio stations the one that sounded "Christian" seemed to intrigue and even captivate me. So I gave it more of a chance and began to listen. I even watched some of the religious programming on television. Today, of course, many televangelists have been discredited for financial or sexual irregularities, even some of the ones I watched in the early 1980s. A few of them fell into sin and lost most of their audiences, and deservedly so. Yet even some of those who fell into sin did preach the gospel of Christ with passion and often with clarity. Some preached in a style I had never been accustomed to, and I confess that I sometimes thought they were more than a little wacky—but their words and delivery drew me to listen, somehow. They seemed convinced, and their confidence made an impact on me. I began to understand the gospel message more and more. You have to understand that I needed time to assimilate all of this. The Protestant Reformer Martin Luther argued in the sixteenth century that saving faith has three elements—knowledge, assent, and trust. You have to have some knowledge, and you have to be able to say, "I believe that this story is true" before you can get to the point where you place all your hope and trust in it for salvation. In early America the Puritans taught that people needed an extended preparation before grace could be received. They believed this preparation would take years, and they seldom accepted that a person could believe and be converted before the age of about eighteen.

Of course that approach seems to replace faith with knowledge in some ways. But I do believe it usually takes some time to understand and make sense of all of this. The amount of time it takes varies from individual to individual. Some persons may hear the message for the first time, give it serious consideration, and then come to a place of faith almost immediately. Others require more time to consider the faith. You may have to be able to work it out in your mind and make an intelligent affirmation of the faith, especially if you are an adult. I also think Martin Luther was correct that a person needs knowledge first, followed by an assent. One must come to the place where one says, "I believe that Jesus did die on the cross so that sinners might be saved." There is no way to trust Christ to save if you don't believe in the facts of the gospel message.

But salvation is never really initiated unless you get past simple affirmation to actual *trust*. Faith is a way of saying, "Grace is for me, and I am reaching out for it." Sometimes faith is misunderstood by people. They think when Christians say they are saved by faith, all they mean is that they are delivered by a mere intellectual event—the event of giving assent to the truths of Christianity. But faith that stops there is never sufficient. A Christian is one who says, "I am placing all of my hope for salvation in what Jesus accomplished for me on the cross and in his resurrection." This is faith leading to salvation—a total resting in what Jesus has done, recognition that we, in our own feeble ways, could never do enough to make ourselves spiritually presentable to God, but that Jesus has done that for us. Then we look to what the Lord has done as our one and only hope for salvation. Like the old song says, a Christian is one who affirms, "My hope is built on nothing less than Jesus' blood and righteousness."

Debbie and I were coming to the point of trust through the process of intellectual and ministry influences I have already described. But like any new seekers, we needed help in finding the truth. Having experienced the need myself, I know now that this help is very, very important. If we simply leave new Christians or near-Christians to develop on their own, they will probably have many more struggles and failures than if someone took responsibility to help and mentor them. This principle works in every area of life, whether business, sports, family, or one's spiritual life. Jesus mentored his disciples. The apostle Paul coached Timothy, as well as several other young men in his entourage. This is a critical matter in every area, and it was central to our spiritual growth.

Thankfully, along the way there were those placed in our path who planted and watered the seed of faith in us. A friend invited us to his church, and as I stood next to him I listened to him sing with an enthusiasm I had never before witnessed at a church service. I realized that he was absolutely convinced not only of the truths he was singing about, but also of the fact that these truths were a reality within his own life. I was deeply moved by his obvious sincerity.

God was after me. Actually, the hound of heaven was after both of us. I began to realize that, even though I was spiritually blind. One of Debbie's friends was a Christian. She invited us to a church service and to her home for dinner, along with some other people from her church. They all spoke confidently of their faith in Christ—but I was turned off by their approach to their faith and their "clubbiness." I was becoming slowly convinced that the Christian set of beliefs was real, but I still was not sure what I thought about Christian people.

Gandhi once said, "I'd be a Christian, if not for the Christians." Perhaps my attitude was not quite that negative toward Christians, and maybe I just did not yet understand what genuine Christians were really like. I had to admit there was something special about them—something I could not yet put my finger on—but something that was still attractive. At the very least they were convinced they had found something that was life-changing. No one knew better than me that I needed something life-changing to happen. I just wanted it to be real, and I wanted it to be right. No one wants to experience conversion only to discover a few years later that the facts don't add up and that the conversion was to a set of beliefs that really cannot be sustained either intellectually or practically. Most of it added up, but there were still some issues about the Christian faith I was not sure about. Josh McDowell tutored me on the Jesus question, but there are other intellectual hurdles to clear in becoming fully convinced that the Christian path is really the one true and ultimate route to heaven. At least it seemed that way to me at the time.

Ever since I was a young boy there were times I was aware of something—someone—trying to get my attention. But when Debbie was diagnosed with MS, I wanted to get to the root of the question of who God really is. I had been working on the answer to that question earnestly since my boss, Oleh, came to my wedding and began encouraging me to find the truth in Christ. In fact he was "mentoring" me to Christ. I had partially solved some of the issues in my reading of Josh McDowell and in responding to the other influences in my life. But I had still not trusted Christ, and so I was in a state of limbo between being spiritually salvaged and helplessly lost. Of course, that state still leaves one lost, and I needed more than that.

But there was still the issue to resolve in my mind about whether Christians were actually doers of the Word or merely just mouthing nice-sounding platitudes about helping people in need and saving the world. The atheist existentialist writer Albert Camus wrote a book in the 1940s called *The Plague*. The story is set in the later Middle Ages at a time when the bubonic plague has broken out in Europe. The two main characters in the book are a priest and an agnostic physician. The priest keeps saying that there is no sense doing anything about the people suffering and dying from the plague, since it was obviously God's will to send the terrible pestilence as a punishment for the sins of the people. The agnostic doctor, on the other hand, gives his life in trying to alleviate pain and suffering. Camus's point is that the people who do something about suffering are not necessarily the religious people, but practical people, even agnostics.

The problem with the book is that it is just a lie. Contrary to some of the propaganda out there, we were discovering that throughout the ages Christians have been and still are taking many steps to alleviate pain and suffering. Look back on the history of philanthropy, and in virtually every area, you will find Christians at work. After her conversion to Christianity, Helena, the mother of Emperor Constantine, built hospitals and hospices all over Europe. It is no coincidence that up until very recent times, most of the hospitals in America were named "St. Somebody," or Baptist, or Presbyterian Hospital. There is a reason for that. Slavery came to an end in England when Christian people like William Wilberforce undertook to end the hated slave trade, and he did it in the name of Christ, not merely in the name of humanity. Amy Carmichael, a Christian missionary to India, did more than any other person of her time to end the childhood prostitution trade in Hindu temples where girls as young as eight years old were being sold out by the priests of the Hindu gods Ganesha and Shiva. In virtually every area—education, women's rights, health care, care for the aged—Christian people have taken the lead in offering practical ministry to those who are in need of it. I did not know of all these examples of active Christian faith at the time God was working on Debbie and me, luring us by various means, but I was coming around to the truth.

Chapter 5

Remolding the Broken Vessel

Escape from Reality

I WAS ANGRY with God. Sometimes I was even angry at Debbie. Had she not contracted this dreaded aliment, my life would have been wonderful, I often thought.

Of course, I knew it was not her fault, but sometimes I could not help feeling resentful. I sometimes even hurled my anger toward my beloved wife—but it was really God and I who were in a wrestling match. Though others who were part of our lives expressed the pity and love they felt toward us, I added a pretty big spoonful of self-pity to the recipe. And I kept fighting, not realizing that the Master Potter was allowing this hardened lump of clay that was Mark Grawehr to be hammered, pressed, pounded and fired by this shattering of my wife and our dream for the future.

Self pity is a tricky thing. When you are feeling sorry for yourself, you often don't even recognize it. Oswald Chambers said, "No sin is worse than the sin of self-pity, because it obliterates God and puts self-interest on the throne." Self-pity arises from the implicit notion that we can somehow be in control of our own lives. That is a false assumption. Only one Person is ultimately in control, and that is the Master Potter. We want to control our lives, but we have to learn at some point that this is just something outside our power to do.

The person who is consumed with self-pity always asks the question, *"Why?"* When he or she is battling with pain and suffering, that is the question in the mind and often on the lips. "Why?" Of course, what that question really means in the heart of a person consumed with self pity is "Why *me?*" Frankly, it would not be so bad if someone else were going through all of this. But why does it have to be *me?* I dealt with that attitude quite a bit at this stage of the illness. I am not proud of it, but it happened, and I can now admit it.

My key escape was going to work—my job. I had always had my agenda, an agenda that was very clear. I wanted to be successful, to have a nice wife, nice house, and all the amenities of the American Dream. At one level I believe there is nothing really wrong with that. Even in the Bible, people who worked hard often were very blessed by God financially. Take a look at a guy like Abraham. When the book of Genesis states that he had 318 servants, that is like commenting that an American businessman has a net worth of several million dollars. Blessed people in the Bible were often (though not always) blessed financially, as well as spiritually. So, there is nothing intrinsically wrong with wanting to make a good living, having nice things, and being successful in business. The problem with me was that I wanted that for all the wrong reasons; I was really very selfish. So then, the effort to work hard and to make a lot of money was what drove me and consumed me in the hours I was not at home with Debbie. The one redeeming factor was that I was often able to work on projects at my home. I did that every chance I could. Yet, it was a diversion and an escape even then.

Then there was my other escape. I searched for tranquility through getting high. Thankfully, I was never addicted to alcohol, though "Mark T Brewer" could sure pound em' down. My mood-altering drug of choice was marijuana. It provided me a break from my intensely driven type-A+ personality. A little weed, here and there, seemed to calm me down and help me zone out into a fun and/or relaxed zombie mode. It did not take long to discover that this was no real escape, but that fact did not keep me from using the drug and trying to elude the craziness of my life.

Cornered by God

As my encounters with Christian literature, radio, and Oleh began really to sink in, God began to reveal to me the ugliness of who I was apart from him. It was not a pretty process. The pounding and the beating out of the air bubbles of pride in the lump of clay named Mark Grawehr was painful, and in spite of what Oleh had told me about God, if this was the process of coming to know him, it did not seem the least bit "loving." I was content being the boss of my own life. Pharaoh asked Moses a question when he urged the Egyptian king to let the Israelites go. "Who is God that I should obey Him?" (Exodus 5:2). I also wanted to know, who is this God allowing this assault to come upon my life? What did I do to deserve this?

Though I was near the point of intellectual assent on the question of whether Jesus really was who (and what) he said he was, I continued to grapple with the concept of whether Jesus was truly God, especially as to how it related to me. I thought God would have a more spectacular plan than coming as a man to die on the cross. And just how could someone be both God and man at the same time? It made little sense. Meanwhile I think God was beginning to answer my prayer—to show me who I was by showing me who he was. In one of the most famous Christian books of all time, *The Institutes of Christian Religion*, John Calvin wrote, "nearly all the wisdom we possess, that is to say, true and sound wisdom, consists of two parts: the knowledge of God and of ourselves." He went on to say that even unbelievers are in some sense searching for God, as out of the misery of their own condition they look for him. "The miserable ruin, into which the rebellion of the first man cast us, especially compels us to look upward." This sense of lostness begins to drive us once the Spirit of God awakens our hearts to our own needs. "Accordingly, the knowledge of ourselves not only arouses us to seek God, but also, as it were, leads us by the hand to find him." That is, we know God by learning of ourselves, and we come to know ourselves by being confronted with the person of God. It is a kind of two-way street (*Institutes of the Christian Religion*).

There was something missing in my life, and I knew it had something to do with the teaching found in the Bible, but I just did not think I was ready to believe *everything* about this gospel message. I did not consider myself to be some kind of intellectual with a logical, air-tight case against the Christian faith, like some Harvard or Cambridge professor with his "Top 10 Reasons Not to Believe the Bible." That was not my problem. I was not arguing against the Bible from some philosophical system. I really did not have a system at the time at all. As I have already noted, I had come to find many things about the faith to be quite sensible and even intellectually appealing. I had even, through the help of Josh McDowell's writings, come to believe intellectually that Jesus was *probably* who the Bible says he was. That was the major part of the battle, but it was not the whole battle. I was simply not quite ready yet to state that I affirmed that all that the Christian gospel states is the real and final truth. I was close, but still, oh, so far away.

By summer 1980 the disease had gained a firm grip. Debbie was unable to walk, feed herself, or speak clearly. A group of Christian people had heard about Debbie's illness and asked permission to come by and pray with her on occasion. Frankly at this point I was open to anything, and I certainly did not think it would hurt. I was at the end of my own tether and was beginning to suspect that what Oleh had to say about Christianity might really be true—all of it, and not just the parts I had come to appreciate from reading and listening to preaching. Although the group typically came when they knew I was out with the guys, one night I was there when they came to pray. They prayed fervently over Debbie. They seemed to be Christians with a very passionate faith and an extreme confidence in God's power. One of the men even told me that God had miraculously placed a gold tooth in his mouth after he had prayed that God would do so! I had my doubts about that then, and still do, but they were sincere people.

From my perspective, this evening began to get really weird! As they prayed, Debbie began to think about the heavy burden of sin and guilt she carried over from issues from her past. She told me she felt a profoundly moving sense of warmth come over her. She experienced a sensation that left her convinced that the hand of God had come on her. To this day I'm still not sure exactly what to make of this. Maybe it was an angel? She acknowledged afterward that she had prayed and trusted Christ alone to save her during that prayer time. She was confident that Christ had done just that.

The days that followed were as if someone had flipped some kind of hidden switch in her heart—one that had never been flipped before. It was as if a component in a piece of equipment had suddenly begun to work, one that had never been operative before. Imagine that you had grown up in a place like Antarctica and had never before seen a field of flowers. Perhaps you had seen a few here and there in the very few days of summer when the snow retreats for a few days from the tundra. Then, you are transported to Holland in the summer and have the chance to gaze at fields filled with tulips, daisies, and other beautiful flowers. The sensation might be like moving from a black-and-white world to one of living color. There was peace on Debbie's countenance and a contentment in her heart that had never been there before, and one that certainly had been absent during the months of her illness. I could tell it. I could see it. It was not just contrived—it was real!

Death was still with Debbie, but she was slowly being freed from its destructive grip. Selfishness, hatred, and pride are all opposed to life and are the marks of death. Love, self-sacrifice, and faith, on the other hand, are all of the very essence of life. Sacrifice now replaced selfishness in Debbie's heart. It is a gift from God to be expressed in life and in relationships. Death would no longer have the last word in Debbie's experience, since she had been freed from its icy snare. While my world still revolved around one person—me—now it seemed she had actually connected with God somehow and that profoundly changed the way she related to others, including me.

You might think that the illness in itself, from the time it began, would have had the immediate result of bringing us closer to each other, but we both had strong wills and behind closed doors we still found ourselves on collision courses. My words flew towards her in those early days of the disease. In our attitudes we spoke things to each other that were like arrows to the heart, eyes glaring, nostrils flaring, lips snarling.

But once the Master Potter freed Debbie from her burden of pride, selfishness and guilt, she suddenly knew the importance of each moment. Having been forgiven of her own sins, she now had the ability and grace from God to forgive me of my sins toward her, especially my verbal sins, my anger. It happens just like that. When you know that you as a person undeserving of forgiveness are forgiven, it engenders such gratitude in your heart that you almost cannot help but forgive those who have wronged you. But I didn't know that from experience as yet.

Now, when I unleashed my frustrations, she no longer looked at me in a distraught manner. Instead she looked at me with eyes of love. When venom came from my lips, grace emerged from hers. When I hurled those piercing arrows of criticism at my precious wife, her gaze of love melted my heart like the hot tropical sun on sheets of ice. She was, in the words of C. S. Lewis, "surprised by joy." And she was not the only one surprised!

It was such a profound change that I was much moved. I began, almost grudgingly, to believe that something supernatural had happened in her life, something that had transformed a suffering, hopeless woman into a person she had never before been. Of course, that is not to say that Debbie had not already had a wonderful and appealing personality. But this was different—this was a quality beyond what she had ever demonstrated, a power that had to come from outside her, transforming her in ways I did not yet understand.

If that was Jesus drawing her to himself, I began to think that I might want that for myself, as well. As I noted above, God's grace often encounters us with conviction of sin, helping us to see just who we really are without Christ. But God's grace also often melts our hearts by its winsomeness. God shows us how beautiful he is, and how beautiful people can become when they have been impacted by his saving grace.

Now I can explain from the other side of grace what was happening with Debbie. Debbie knew she was becoming one of God's own special works, but she longed for me to have the same experience. She longed for me to know the life-transforming peace of heart and the soul-soothing balm of knowing Christ as Savior, of experiencing his forgiveness, and of having the confidence of life eternal. It was as though a river of peace flowed from her mind and body. The beauty of that peace slowly but surely overcame the barbarism that still lurked in my heart. Her gentle spirit reversed my river of built-up rage. Her soft look crushed my strongly barricaded walls of selfish anger and caused my impenetrable fortress of pride to begin to crumble.

God's incredible strength poured through her weakened body and gentle heart, as she knew now that God had placed her sin on Christ and punished that sin on the cross. As a result she had received the gift of forgiveness and salvation. All she wanted was to love. Prideful defense could have been hurled back with a glare, yet as she gazed on Jesus, she would no longer return my anger in kind, but instead let his beauty pour forth from her. My sweetheart, like Jesus before her, entrusted herself and the remainder of her life to the heavenly Father. This was an incredible change and it occurred right before my eyes. I had no way to explain it other than that some supernatural force had transformed my bride from the inside out.

I was at a crisis, a crossroads in my life. I knew the pain of guilt over my sin. I knew that I had failed everyone around me in many ways because of my anger, my selfishness, and my unforgiving heart. But I told myself that MS was to blame, not me. Like a thief that breaks into a quiet, well-kept home and turns it into a shambles before taking everything of value, it had robbed me of any possibility of hopefulness for the future. It had halted me in my tracks.

My bitterness toward God, as much as I knew him to be God at that time, soured everything else in my life. I knew that I was being destroyed, not just by my wife's illness, but also by my guilt over both my past rebellion and over the way I was handling my life then and there. I knew I needed something, and that something was what I now saw in my beautiful bride—that transformation of demeanor, that release from the past, that confident expectation for the future. She had it, and I did not. I wanted it. But at the same time I was afraid to want it. This was a scary moment for me.

One night I said to her, "I am still not sure that Jesus is everything Scripture paints him out to be, but I suspect he might be. I am not sure about everything in the Bible. Please pray that it will become clear to me." She could still speak a little at that time, though her voice was garbled and jittery. But the words she spoke and the look on her countenance made it clear that she would be praying for me. In fact, I know she prayed for me a lot.

In the Potter's Hands

Debbie was in and out of the hospital in the late summer and fall of 1980. On one occasion her fever was very high, and though she protested, I forced her to go. She indicated she would be just fine through self-medication, but I would not hear it, and to the hospital we went. I determined I would stay with her overnight in case she needed me. The nurses said they had to get her temperature down, so they put her in an ice blanket. The controls on the blanket indicated that they had not yet reduced her fever, but I could tell she was getting colder and colder. Though I knew little about the medical technique they were employing, something did not seem right. I pointed out that her hands and feet were getting very cold. The nurses said she was fine. Somehow I knew they were wrong, and I urged them again to consider whether her body was getting too cold.

Medical people often have to deal with interfering family members during procedures, and sometimes those family members can become a nagging problem keeping the staff from doing their duty. That is what they obviously thought of me, and they blew me off as a complainer. "Don't bother us, we know what we are doing," they snapped, in so many words. I replied, "I don't think the control is working—she is getting too cold." I finally walked out and went to the desk and said, "This is not working right." A doctor came in and took a look.

He immediately put in an urgent call to the head nurse. Stat! People were suddenly scurrying everywhere to get her temperature back up to normal. I was angry. I was trying to be a good husband—to do the right thing. She feared going to the hospital, but I had made her go, and my insistence had almost cost Debbie her life.

When we came home, her fever problem seemed to have departed. A day or two later, however, she again had a high fever while lying on the couch. Her eyes then rolled back into her head—I could only see the whites of her eyes. I picked her up and carried her into the bedroom and laid her on the bed. She was clammy and limp. Here was my captain of the twirlers, my homecoming queen, my bride, lying in a helpless state in my arms. I felt in many ways even more helpless than she was. Do I take her back to the hospital and risk another potential disaster? Would she come out of the fever and her state of unconsciousness and be fine again in a short while? I was upset, angry, indecisive, and terrified! Debbie was lying there helplessly, and there seemed to be no right and clear course of action for me to take. I just flopped onto the bed and cried for the first time since I was a kid.

I was a "fix-it" guy, but I couldn't fix this. Suddenly I realized my whole attitude was one of pure selfishness. I lay there with my face in my pillow, calling out softly but desperately to God, "If you are really there and if Jesus is really your Son, help me to believe that." I was weeping, softly at first as I struggled to maintain control of my senses and my pride. Then, as I became overwhelmed by the weight of my selfishness, I began sobbing quite intensely.

I now realized I had been at the center of my little universe. I recognized that it was wrong to live like that and that somehow we were placed here for a reason, part of which was to live for others and not merely ourselves. I had tried to do better and be better since my wife became ill, but somehow I had not been able to pull it off. I now faced the fact that I not only had not been successful in conquering myself, but that fundamentally I was incapable of doing so. I needed a Savior. I needed both the grace that forgives and the grace that transforms. I needed to be cleansed and ultimately I needed to be a different person.

The North African church father Augustine had similarly tried to make himself a better man and so earn the reward for the righteous life. By the age of thirty-two Augustine had been trying to live a righteous existence and "save himself" for half of his life, moving from one philosophy to another in a vain hope of making sense of the world around him. Then one day he read the passage in the letter to the Romans where Paul had written, "Not in riots and drunken parties, not in eroticism and indecencies, not in strife and rivalry, but put on the Lord Jesus Christ and make no provision for the flesh in its lusts" (Romans 13:13-14—this rendering is from a translation of the *Confessions* by Henry Chadwick, Oxford University Press, 1991). Salvation came not by Augustine's efforts, but by the efforts of Christ.

He needed a Savior, one who accomplished the work of redemption for him, so that what he had to do was to "put on" that Savior. I also needed a Savior. The Christian faith suddenly made sense to me. Jesus died for me—me who needed all he had to give. I had not struggled with these issues for as long as Augustine had, but I had certainly been plunged into a crash course in what life can throw at you. At that moment it seemed as though I was at a milestone in coming to grips with the truth that a loving God had somehow grasped our lives. We were in his strong and loving hands. He would mold us into his image and he was not about to let us go.

Much happened in those moments with my face in the pillow. I was confronted with a set of truths I had not prepared myself to address, but there it was. I now realized I was not in control of my world, but I knew who was. My wife was still very ill and she might not get better, but somehow that was not as frightening as it had been only a few moments before. More than that, I now knew that I had come face to face with God, God in the person of Jesus. I knew that the one I had once rejected I could reject no more.

Scripture teaches that before we come to Christ and trust him as Savior we are at war with God—Romans 8:7 says, "the sinful mind is hostile to God." Whatever people may say about how they really love the Lord and with what friendly terms they are on with him, those who have not come to Christ in faith actually set themselves as enemies of the one true and living God. And they remain enemies until the day they lose the battle and the conflict ceases. For me, the battle against God was finally over. I had lost the war, and what a glorious defeat it was. There would be many more battles to come in the next several years, different kinds of battles, but the way to victory in those battles had now been made possible for me, since I was defeated in the most crucial battle of all—my personal battle against God.

On that October day God revealed himself to me as never before. The Master Potter brought quiet to my inner heart-wrenching pain with the reality that he was following his own eternal plan that I was now beginning to see, though still only dimly. The light of Christ within me now for the first time was flickering with warmth and giving me glimpses of God's magnificence. This glory and majesty would eventually burst forth through the shards of married life. Somehow I knew that was about to happen, though I did not yet understand exactly how.

It was as though the forest fire that was raging in my mind was now being doused with the refreshing water that Jesus said would pour forth from those who came to him (John 7). There was an internal calm and peace in my life that I had never known. I did not have all the answers, nor would I ever have them all, but a small light in my mind began to make sense of the chaos we had known all these months.

I realized for the first time that there was a real sovereign Being intricately involved in my life. As I became aware of that, I also recognized that this divine visitor was now in the process of replacing my jealousy with grace, my selfishness with a passion to serve, and my anger with contentment. It did not happen all at once, but it *began* to happen all at once. I was aware all of a sudden that there was a Reality in my life that had not been there before, at least not consciously to me, and I was also aware that I could not imagine being without that Reality ever again.

Centuries before Jesus came to earth David prayed, "Do not. . .take your Holy Spirit from me" (Psalm 51:11). I did not yet know what or who the Holy Spirit was, and in fact I did not know where in the Bible that passage came from, but I knew I did not want ever again to be without the Person I was now learning to know. Nor did I realize that once his life became alive in me that this life, because of what Jesus did on the cross, would never be rescinded. Jesus said that no one could ever snatch his people out of the Father's hand or out of his (Jesus') hand (John 10:27-30). The apostle Paul affirmed this very truth when he argued that nothing can ever separate us from the love of God if we are truly his children. He then enumerated a list of things that people might think could alienate them from God, concluding that *nothing* "in all creation. . .will be able to separate us from the love of God that is in Christ Jesus our Lord" (Romans 8:39). Nothing and no one—not even ourselves—can ever snatch us away from God's love or out of the hand of the Father.

Probably the greatest confidence I had was that God had forgiven me. Me! As I have stated all along, I was painfully aware of my shortfalls. I tried to forget them. I tried to rationalize them away by saying that others were worse than I was. But believe me when I say that I had wrestled with guilt for years. Nevertheless, now my sin was forgiven. It is difficult to explain the inner change that was taking place in my heart, but it was so evident to me at the time. I knew this was the defining moment of my life. Everything else would be a footnote to this experience.

Up to this point I had wallowed in the self-pity of thinking that my entire future had been washed away in a sea of disease and all that accompanied it. God gave me a whole new vision for our life together. Like a light instantly shining, it illuminated my shattered plans with a gentle reassurance that the sovereign God has a plan that dwarfs any I could ever have imagined. Human ingenuity can never match God's purposes because humans can't see the world on the same scale.

I now knew that God brought us to this place in our lives because he had something for us to do. That something would include my professional career and the opportunities it would bring, but it would not end there. I knew that the Lord was calling us to a place of faith in him, but I also knew God would provide the way. We are mere jars of clay, mud pots molded and shaped by the Father to become vessels for his use. Along the way we need to remind ourselves that there is no inherent value in this clay itself. It is simply mud. The great value comes as we are transformed by the Master Potter into useful vessels for service in the Kingdom. In my view that in a nutshell is the secret of life.

Transformed into a New Vessel

I pushed myself away from my pillow, wondering if Debbie might live or die. But when I looked at her, she smiled a bit and trembled out the word, "hungry." The fever was gone. Debbie was going to live through another day. This word deeply moved me. Was this some kind of miracle? To this day I'm not exactly sure. But God used it, at minimum in his timing, as confirmation of what I had wrestled through in my encounter with him. God is truly real and does care very much about us. That is a truth that can sometimes only really be learned in the crucible of pain and suffering. It is a truth Debbie and I knew at that very moment to be exactly the case.

That day in 1980 God drew me to himself by showing his hand in all we were going through. As the lifting of a fog along a coastline shows exactly what was there but had been unseen, the spiritual fog that clouded my vision now lifted so that I could see the working of

God in Debbie's illness. As the fog that clouded everything else in my previous life lifted, I began to see things more clearly, and all the more so as the days passed.

Scripture began to really come alive. The truths of the faith unfolded before me and it was clear that they made perfect sense. It is at least partly true that the truth of Christianity never becomes completely real to you until you commit yourself in faith to the Lord. Thomas Aquinas, a theologian from the Middle Ages, once said, "I understand, in order that I may believe." In his view, understanding precedes faith. That is partly true, and of course, I had been trying to understand things like the deity of Christ by the reading I was doing. But another thinker from the Middle Ages, Anselm, stated, "I believe in order that I may understand." I think Anselm's analysis is a little bit closer to the way it really is. God had been at work in our lives all along but after turning this corner, things in our life together would never be the same!

I now had a new and a deep hunger for the Bible. I hung on every word. I did not *understand* every word, but it was like water to a thirsty man for me. My mind was filled with so many new things; it was as if I was discovering new lands and new scenery every day in my searching of God's Word. Scripture is the major tool, though not the only one, by which we come to know the Lord. It tells us who he is and what he has done on our behalf. I wanted to know everything it was possible for me to know. I drank it in, and every day God showed me something new about him, and something new about myself, as well. That was both good and bad!

Over the following days as Debbie and I tried to reorient our lives around our new-found Savior, he began to bring together the shattered fragments of our hearts. The pain we had inflicted on each other, and especially the pain I had poured out on her, began now to be transformed to something else. It was transformed into a living testimony of what God can do in the hearts of people.

Aside from Debbie's illness, we were pretty normal people. But normal people, like us, are broken people in many ways. Our situation was only different because we faced a spiritual crisis under the duress of another crisis—a profound illness. In that way, our situation was crystallized in certain ways by the sharpness of our difficulty, but we found Christ, or rather, he found us, in pretty much the same way as most. But the following days found us with a passion for him to really remake us both as individuals and as a couple.

Relieved from the burden of guilt and shame, I wanted to explain this life-changing process with friends and family. I wanted to share my new-found faith with others. I had a sudden boldness in this that I could not explain, not even to myself.

I also told our friends, and as a result, we lost most of them. I have grieved about that loss many times since then. I don't think I suddenly became an obnoxious Bible-thumper. I sure didn't want to be. We lost many friends both because my wife's condition changed the dynamics of what it was like to spend time with us and because most of them could not understand our new faith. Our desire to understand and know Christ better made many of our friends uncomfortable. There was nothing I could do about that. But we did feel increasingly isolated. This was hard and added more hurt to an already painful situation. It was an isolation based on Debbie's condition and on our new faith in Jesus Christ. The Holy Spirit now began to fill the God shaped void within our souls. Now I was beginning to learn that my substance abuse was my futile attempt to meet this need. Only later would I begin to realize that countless other prevalent abuses evident in our society ranging from eating habits to sexual addictions merely mask the symptoms of this deeper unmet need.

But of course we did not lose *all* our friends. We had been adopted into a new *family*, and we built some early and wonderful relationships with people around us who loved the Lord. We found encouragement from these new friends, and we also found our "faith muscle" pumped up by reading Scripture and by having fellowship with others who had been found by God in the midst of their own tragedies and challenges. We entered the fellowship of the saints—and by "saints" I mean, as the apostle Paul did in his many uses of the word—other believers and followers of Christ, not merely extraordinary people who had died centuries before. We found that the greatest friendships were yet to come. Most importantly, we knew that we now had fellowship with God, and that he would never let us go.

Debbie was especially impacted by my conversion. She was grateful to God that her prayers had been answered. She was amazed at what she began to see in my life as the Lord was reorienting my entire inner self so I might honor him with all that I did. And I also think that deep down inside, she knew I could now rise to the hard task of caring for her by drawing on God's strength to enable me to do what he called me to do. Most importantly, my wife was grateful to God that her husband had now come to know the God in whom is life eternal. Nothing was, and is, more important than that.

Chapter 6

The Refiner's Fire

~~~

Seeking a New Community of Faith

I WAS ON fire for the Lord from the very beginning. Scripture teaches that when a person places faith in Christ for salvation, that person becomes "a new creation," in the words of 2 Corinthians 5:17. Being a Christian does not merely mean that one has a different eternal point of destination—heaven—though that is certainly true. Being a Christian entails a change of life in every conceivable way. It is not that you get new DNA, but in virtually every other way your life is different. This is especially the case with adult converts, with people who had grown accustomed to viewing life through one set of lenses but who now view it through an entirely different set.

Now I was finding myself hungry for anything that would feed my faith. Like a spiritual sponge, soaking it all in, I continued to read Christian literature voraciously. Life for me was quickly becoming very different—a *good* kind of different. There was emerging within me a new sense of life as I was personally sensing God's presence and care in a powerful way! Now what Debbie was experiencing was perfectly clear to me. Her prayer was answered.

This was no mere fairy-tale type crutch. Actually, though, the *crutch* part was partly right. Somehow, in the providence of the Master of the universe, we were brought to a place of realizing our need. We were genuinely humbled as we began to see things as they really were. But it was no make-believe, false kind of reality thing. No, this was very real. Weird, at first, but real. We were now sharing a personal walk with God together through the very much alive person of Jesus Christ!

But as new believers we faced challenges that often cause even mature Christians to struggle with doubt and despair. We needed a caring community of believers to stand with us and support us through our struggles. Christians need fellowship with other believers, and this is especially the case for new Christians. We needed the support that we could draw from those who had been in the faith longer than we had been. We needed pastoral care and we needed the accountability that comes with being linked together with the same people day in and day out. To be sure, we probably needed that more than many other Christians due to the uniqueness of our situation. We needed a church that we could call our own.

How, though? To be a member of a church, one typically goes to a common meeting place where the congregation gathers. That would be a problem for us. It was extremely difficult to transport Debbie anywhere, even in these early days of the MS, and it was getting more difficult with every month that went by. This was a source of real frustration for both of us and for several reasons. We were increasingly cut off more and more from our old friends and now we were finding it difficult to make new friends with people who shared our values and our faith since we were largely isolated in our home. Deb's mom was always there when I needed her assistance and she called every day. My mom was nearby, too, and reached out to help support us on many occasions. But we longed for a church, Christian people with whom we could fellowship and with whom we could share our struggles and difficulties, as well as our successes and victories.

We ended up joining a radio church. The pastor, a cool old hippie type and fellow child of the 1960s, really ministered to us with sound biblical teaching over the air waves. His church would send us weekly video tapes of the service. I also listened to other radio and TV ministries. Although we were still not connected to a church family in the usual sense of that term, we were at least being fed and ministered to. That was a real help in those early days of our Christian experience.

Speaking Without Words

About a year and a half into our marriage Debbie began losing not just her ability to form words but her voice itself. The loss was not completely unexpected, but it was a blow, nonetheless. The disease had already created certain distances between us because of the difficulty of communication, but now it appeared that communication might be primarily a one-way street. I knew I could not let this happen. All of the other factors made life difficult enough for her. I was determined not to allow her to be forced into a kind of unnatural solitary confinement for the rest of her life. The disease itself was a big enough Goliath; I would not allow a second giant of isolation to bully her into despair.

Since her hearing remained good, I knew that I could communicate with her, even if her condition became so deteriorated that all she could do was blink or make a sound. When her speech began to fail, she still had some use of her fingers and hands, and could make signs to me. But soon she lost that as well. So I created a chart organized into several categories including comfort, hygiene, entertainment, food, and drink. As we laboriously communicated, Debbie would attempt to signal with a blink that meant *yes*, and a stare that meant *no*. Her limited ability to perform those simple signals made understanding Debbie's needs somewhat possible, but very tedious. And it was a far from foolproof system because at times even early in her illness her blinking was difficult for her to control.

So when I knew she needed something or when I was simply trying to "talk" to her, I would use one of the category words. If I would use the word "entertainment," and she indicated "yes," I had further options. I would ask "radio"? If yes, then AM or FM? If no, I would ask "TV"? If yes, then I would go through the options of what was on television at that time. If she indicated no to TV, I would ask her if she would like me to read to her, and so on. We would do the same thing with hunger and thirst and other personal needs. So, for instance, under "comfort," I might ask "hot or cold"? Or I would ask her about whether her upper body was in a good or bad position, or did it have to do with lower body, did she wish to lean back or lean forward, and so on.

If it wasn't on the chart we simply went to the spell option but this was even slower and more tedious. As the years went by and her debilitation increased, this chart became increasingly necessary for us to keep the lines of communication open. In general it was a good system for awhile. But then as her ability to even control her blinking failed it became unbearably frustrating. But that was still quite a bit in the future.

Debbie had always been extremely mindful of her physical appearance. So she was always careful about her diet to avoid becoming overweight, along with everything else. She would berate herself mentally if she "cheated" on her diet, and when she was still able to feed herself and keep up her journal she would record, for instance, that she had eaten a tiny sliver of cheese cake when it was really not on her list of things she allowed herself to eat. She would write, "I cheated. I hate myself for that."

As nearly all of life's simple joys became just a memory, eating remained as one of her few pleasures, so we did what we could to provide her special requests. She loved brussels sprouts, cabbage, baked egg plant, and pesto—and her ultimate favorite was ice cream. Her swallowing mechanism also began to be affected, so there were many things she could not eat in a normal way. Still, you might be surprised how much pleasure a person who has lost the ability to chew and swallow might get out of tasting pepperoni pizza or a cheeseburger pureed up in a kitchen blender. The thought may be a little repulsive, since most of us do not run a steak or baked potato through a blender, but what else could we do? Actually Debbie was almost always very disciplined and demonstrated incredible willpower, as she generally stuck to a very healthy, but not so delicious, culinary regime. As her chief nutritional coach, commissioned with enforcing the specialist's recommendations, I must say that it pleased me greatly when she was able to find some pleasure at meal times.

Despite all the precautions she continued to have infections. The doctors recommended a urinary catheter, but Debbie passionately declared her objection to that. She wanted neither a urinary catheter nor a feeding tube. Having been a nurse to patients with this illness, she knew that those options would be proposed at some point in the process. What we were facing was the increasing "progression" of the disease. (Isn't it amazing how we sometimes use the word *progression?*) I had to think about two things at once. One of those had to do with the recommendations coming from her doctors. Though I was not always convinced they were giving us good advice, I did understand they knew what they were talking about most of the time, and that I should take their suggestions seriously.

At the same time, and secondly, I had to consider my bride's self-respect, dignity, and sense of well being. I often felt myself torn between these two opposing forces. If the doctors convinced me that a course of action was necessary to preserve her life, I would try to persuade Debbie that this was the best way to go, even if it was going to be hard for her. She always left the final decision with me. That very fact made me very deliberate when it came to starting a new kind of treatment or adding any new technology to deal with her condition.

It was becoming clear that this thing, this uninvited guest, was becoming more and more invasive in her body and in our relationship. The Master Potter was molding each of our lives—we had no doubt about that. But each of us had to function in our unfinished "jars of clay," our physical bodies, as best we knew how. For us, the new problems further pounded out the "flesh," our own agendas, helping us further to try to live in God's own supernatural power and love.

I knew that I needed the fullness of God's Spirit in my life in order to function and to lead my wife. I was learning how to lean on Christ, and to depend on him for direction as well as for strength. God enabled me to begin loving my wife with his kind of love, not my worldly or self-centered kind of love. God was changing my heart, that I knew, but it was not an immediate sort of thing.

One in Christ and One in Flesh

"No discipline seems pleasant at the time," says Hebrews 12:11. Discipline trains us up to be what God wants us to be. But discipline is often difficult, whether it is the discipline of *training* or the discipline of *chastisement*, and both of these are aspects of discipline. Both kinds shape us. Despite the fact that we needed the chart to communicate, and despite the fact that I was forced to be the nurse in the evenings, in Christ

I really was learning to become to Debbie what she needed in a husband. I was now ready to serve the Master through her in that way.

Essentially, I was Debbie's arms and legs, and I grew in a love relationship with her that was so close that as she was hurting, I was also hurting. As Christ identified with us in our weakness by becoming flesh and thereby redeeming us, so God was helping me to identify with my wife's condition and to become one with her as her hands, legs, and eyes. There is a song written by Joni Eareckson Tada that says, "May I borrow your hands—mine don't work so well." How she spurred us along through the years with her comforting words as one who had been further along on the journey than us. God moved my heart, mind and body towards an incredible oneness, growing deeper in identifying with Debbie's weakness and hurt.

The depth of my love for Debbie increased as I continued to see Christ in her responses to it all. The depth of my love for Christ increased as I increasingly saw his presence revealed within this precious jar of clay. Scripture speaks of this awesome principle in 2 Corinthians 4:7, 9:

> But we have this treasure in jars of clay to show that this all-surpassing power is from God and not from us. We are hard pressed on every side, but not crushed; perplexed, but not in despair; persecuted, but not abandoned; struck down, but not destroyed.

Paul says the glory is actually increasing in jars that are fading, "though outwardly we are wasting away, yet inwardly we are being renewed day by day" (4:16). Actually, the treasure is precious and has the unsurpassed glory of Christ surrounding it. The jar of clay is precious in the sense that it contains the "ministry," as Paul calls it, of "the light of the knowledge of the glory of God in Jesus Christ" (4:6).

This light is the image of God, and it radiates from our clay jars. We offer ourselves in service to Christ so that the life of Jesus may be revealed in our bodies, yet even that offering is something God has already given to us. God does not really need us, but in his mercy he has given to us the right and the power to give ourselves to him. Of course, those who are not yet the children of God don't begin to understand this. It is foolishness to those who do not know God, even as the cross is foolishness to those who are spiritually dying (1 Corinthians 1:18). The god of this age, Satan, has blinded their hearts and minds so that they "cannot see the light of the glory of the gospel of Christ" (2 Corinthians 4:4).

What about us? The apostle Paul says we have mercifully received the ministry of the Spirit. He also notes that, just as in Genesis when God declared, "Let there be light," so that light might overcome the darkness, in our lives God's glorious light shines out of us, out of these jars of clay. That light shines in the darkness of this world. What this means is that our sufferings, our momentary afflictions, enable us to join God in making the world more and more a world of light (2 Corinthians 4:17). It is creating an eternal weight of glory.

That happens primarily as we endure pain and suffering for the sake of Christ. He gives us this treasure in jars of clay. Why? To demonstrate that the incomparable all-surpassing power is not from us, but from the Person and the Power who indwell us. We are empowered as we reflect the ministry of God's glory in the midst of our troubles, from an eternal perspective. All of this means, I learned, that we should let the Light shine through us as we minister.

Very few people reading this book will have ever observed Debbie and me together as husband and wife. What I would like for you to know is that we really *were* husband and wife. Maybe you are thinking this is a story about a man whose wife was ill, and who then had to give his life taking care of her, functioning as a nurse but not much as a husband. I did of course have to take care of her—a challenging task—but more than anything else, ours is a story of two people who loved each other very much as husband and wife. Because we found a way to communicate with each other even after she lost the ability to speak, it was possible, even if arduous, for her to "talk" to me.

And from my side this is a story of love and commitment that began with the usual kind of passion that brings people together into marriage, but which continued with an increased and matured passion over the years we were together. Our intimacy increased with passion and maturity and insight; even though the outward man was perishing daily, the inner man was being renewed day by day (2 Corinthians 4:12-18). This was true for both Debbie and me over the years we shared together.

I can only express myself here with words that are plain and direct. *I loved Debbie.* Let me try to unpack that statement. Even before I was a Christian believer, I wanted to do the best for my wife—to go beyond myself for her. As a self-centered person, I was not always consistent in my efforts, but I knew that was what I wanted to be like, even when I failed in the attempt.

Now as a Christian, I had the resources from the Lord to make that more and more into a reality. Due to her illness, though, I had a much greater challenge before me in helping her to be happy, fulfilled, and comfortable. Those are legitimate desires. God designed us with the capacity for contentment and joy and with the expectation that, all other things being equal, we would find those things in life. There is nothing wrong and everything right with being joyful in good circumstances. But this really becomes a gift from God when things get rough. One of the goals in marriage is helping one another find those qualities. The goal is a two-way street, with husbands fulfilling one role and wives another—and both of them serving one another as they discover joy in a joint commitment.

As months and years passed, however, I realized that there were severe practical limitations on what I could do to make those goals and desires into realities in her life. It seemed clear to us, for instance, that Debbie would not be a mother. That was a limitation on what I could give her—something that most husbands want for their wives and something that most husbands help them to accomplish. Of course she felt the limitation from her side even more severely, that she could not give me children.

There were other limitations, as well. She would no longer be able to prepare meals for me. Like many other wives, she had found pleasure in cooking her husband's favorite foods. She experienced the joy that comes when you prepare a meal especially for someone and then take pleasure in that person's pleasure as he or she enjoys the flavors, the colors, and the smells associated with something as simple as eating a meal. Now those days were gone.

These were only two of the normal things wives do to find joy and contentment and to bring that same joy to their husbands. Two "normal" things which were not to be normal for us. That filled me with anguish, but it also filled me with a resolve to find other ways in which I could help my Beeba find a sense of joy and contentment in her life with me. I also wanted to find ways where she could make a contribution to our relationship together so that she would have the joy not only of receiving but also of giving. I wanted that so much for her.

In the long hours we would spend together, as I would study the lines of her face and the posture of her increasingly tortured body, I asked myself a question again and again. "How can I help her to know my love and how can I help bring joy to her?" I longed to bring joy to her, for whom joy would seem to be an elusive thing. Emerging from my day of work and toil in the fast lane of life, when I got home, what I wanted to do was to bring a smile to her face, to let her know that she was the most important thing in this life to me.

This kind of affection was something given to me by the indwelling Lord who is the Spirit and who was transforming me "from glory to glory" (2 Corinthians 3:18). Increasingly, it replaced my earlier self-centeredness. All I can say is that this transformation was a gift. It was a gift to be able to love my wife the way she deserved to be loved, and also in the way I ought to have loved her. It was a gift from God, one of the many ways where my new existence in Christ was being accomplished to help conform me, mold me, into the kind of person I was to become but had not yet become. It was a work in progress, and part of it was to teach me to love my wife and to desire and work for the best for her in every conceivable way.

Let me make one thing very clear. Debbie was not a difficult person to love. Especially since her conversion, but even to a large degree before, she was such an easy person to please. She appreciated little things and found great joy when I gave her very simple expressions of love and affection. My wife was in no way a "high maintenance" wife emotionally, even though her profound illness made physical maintenance an increasing challenge. When I spoke simple words of affection to her, she smiled broadly with a beautiful and engaging smile. When I brought her foods she really enjoyed, it was as though her entire day had been filled with light.

Along with this came an emotional passion for Debbie that grew in intensity in my heart. It is the right and normal thing for husbands and wives to grow in their feelings for one another over the years. This is a huge issue in marriages. Relationships generally begin with lots of raging hormones and romantic impulses. You want to be with that person all the time to hug, to kiss, to gaze at each other. And of course most people want even more than that, even though most of them have been taught that "more than that" ought to wait for a wedding ring. You just love that person and you want to be with him or her all of the time. That was the way it had been between Debbie and me. Before we were married, I thought about her all the time. I memorized every curve of her face and body. I wanted to kiss her face and hold her next to me. I guess we were just like nearly every other couple about to be married.

After the honeymoon, over time, some of the intensity of all of that begins to wear down. Now you are sleeping with each other every night. The novelty of it begins to be a little less intriguing. In addition, you discover that this person you are married to has some flaws you never noticed before. A woman may have never dreamed that her fiancée actually sometimes belches. Now she sees the other side. After six months of married life she may begin to believe her new husband is something of a cross between Homer Simpson and Attila the Hun!

For his part, the husband may have never thought before just how long it takes a woman to get ready to leave the house, and especially how long she spends in the bathroom. He may start nagging at her about little things. She may become upset at the fact that she has to ask him three times to take out the trash, and then the day comes when he forgets, and before he can get the garbage can out to the street, the trash truck has come and gone. They now have to put up with the smell of that ever-mounting pile of garbage for another whole week! Romance may not be dead, but it has definitely taken a turn for the worse—sometimes a smelly turn!

Over time most couples work through those kinds of issues and they learn they can still retain the romance of their relationship in spite of the complexities and stresses of marriage, not to mention in spite of one another. There are very few marital problems that cannot be solved with a little patience and understanding, and maybe a few thousand dollars in counseling fees!

Seriously, though, millions of married couples experience joy and fulfillment in their relationship together and to one degree or another they also accomplish what I have been talking about here—helping one another find joy. They do it through mutual service one to the other. I think Debbie's frustration was in her inability to do much of anything at all to be a blessing to me. I could recognize on her beautiful face the agony over how difficult she knew it would be for her to demonstrate her love for me in pragmatic ways.

I was learning to love my Beeba in ways that mirrored Christ's love for his bride, as Paul's metaphor often characterizes the church. Both Paul and the book of Revelation picture the church as the *bride* or the *wife* of Christ. In Revelation 19:7–10 we find that at the time of the second coming of Christ there will be a great wedding feast, one for Christ and his bride, the church. The marriage feast of the Lamb appears to be one of consummation as the union between Christ and the church enters a state of uninterrupted fellowship. Sin is finally put away forever, and Christ at that time will be permanently in the physical presence of his bride.

In Ephesians 5:22-33 we find a similar set of ideas, though the author develops the concept more elaborately. Paul writes that in the marriage relationship, the husband should love his wife as Christ loves the church, and that the wife should follow her husband's leadership in a way similar to the church following Christ. I have used the term "metaphor" here, but the relationship as Paul describes it seems to be much more than simply a figure of speech or analogy. Even as Christ and the church are in vital and indivisible union with one another, so a husband and a wife exist in a union that is likewise unbreakable.

The apostle Paul says some extraordinary things in this passage. "For the husband is the head of the wife as Christ is the head of the church, his body, of which he is the Savior" (Ephesians 5:23). Of course the husband is not his wife's spiritual savior; men and women are all saved in the same way, by grace through faith in Jesus. As apostle Paul states, "there is neither. . . male nor female, for you are all one in Jesus Christ" (Galatians 3:28; Ephesians 2:8-10). Granting that, it is still an amazing statement that the husband is given the role of leading and loving his wife in a way that is something like the leadership and love that Christ exercises in reference to the body of Christ, the church. It is astonishing if you just think about it.

What does this entail? For one thing, the husband must love his wife with a sacrificial love. As I have said before, love is not an emotion or a feeling, but is instead an action. The evangelist Charles Finney wrote a book over a hundred years ago entitled, *Love Is Not a Way of Feeling*. He was exactly right. Love does things for others. It does not simply *feel*.

Not only does a husband do things for his wife out of love for her; he does them to the point where it requires sacrifice on his part. This is not hard to understand. Every man does some things for his wife. Most men go to work every week, and at least part of that choice is out of consideration to support his wife and family. Even if he is not the only breadwinner in the household, he still does this out of love for his wife. But if you think about it, there is not a great deal of sacrifice in simply going to work. It is a basic requirement of life that most of us must work to earn the daily bread that goes on the table.

Even as far back as the time of creation, God gave Adam work to do. After he sinned, he was told that now his work would be done "by the sweat of his face" and that he would toil against "thorns and thistles." In other words, his work would now often be difficult and challenging (Genesis 3:17-19). Adam's rebellion meant that one day he would die, but it also meant that the very world in which he lived was tarnished and fallen. In a fallen world, work is often difficult, but it is still a basic component of one's life. Because work sometimes is sacrificial, it must be the case that a husband loving his wife sacrificially must do more than simply earn her a living. That is simply one of the baby steps of love.

How did Christ, the head of the church, love the church with a sacrificial love? Two things are obvious: He lived for her, and he died for her. As prophesized, Christ was born of a virgin to deliver his people. He lived out his physical existence for the church and he continues to do so. It was God's purpose for all fullness to dwell in Jesus so that through the Son the Father might "reconcile to himself all things" (Colossians 1:19–20). Before the incarnation, that is, before Jesus took humanity for himself, the Son of God never knew suffering or pain. He was never hungry, thirsty, or weary, and he never had any kind of physical ailments. But he took on the human form and nature for himself, and he lived for his bride every day. Out of obedience to the Father who called the Son to the task, Jesus lived every day before being *crucified* for the people the Father sent him to rescue (Matthew 1:21).

But the story does not end there. He continues to live every day in his resurrected body, and this is for the sake of the church as well. The writer to the Hebrews states that even now Jesus "always lives to intercede for" his church. Since Jesus was also tempted in his earthly life (Hebrews 2:18; 7:25), he is able to come to our aid when we are tempted. He came in the first century to serve his bride, and he continues to live for the sake of this bride into the twenty-first century. In this way Jesus is preparing Christians for the great wedding feast we see in the book of Revelation.

Paul's teaching in the fifth chapter of Ephesians about husbands loving their wives as Christ loved the church means a husband loves his wife by living for her. I did not learn these things immediately, and I did not have it all down in 1980. But God started to teach me and I was starting to get it. I knew that when I made my wife's bed at night, when I took pains to dress her carefully in the morning and do everything else that was part of our life together, all of it was something that was part of the mystery of marriage. More than that, it was part of the mystery of Christ.

In some sense, I believe I was living out my union with Christ by living out my union with Debbie. A major part of that union with Debbie meant that I was called to love her by living my life for her. She became the physical, tangible focus of my life and of all that I did and all that I was. There were other components of my life, of course—work, friends, church—but all of them took second place to my wife, who became the focus of my concerns and attentions.

In a sense, I was thrown into the mystery of marriage by circumstances. I literally had to live my life for my wife because it was the only real way she could have a life with any kind of quality at all. I was far from perfect in my care for her in many ways. But I could have resisted caring for her. I could have turned her over to professional nurses. I could have distanced myself from her emotionally and spiritually because the challenge was so difficult and so very daily. Other husbands have done so. But God would not let me go that way. Actually, it was not even an option. The mystery of Christ and the mystery of the church would not let me. She became my life, and that is as it ought to have been.

What about husbands whose wives do not have some debilitating illness? Should they also live their lives for their wives as Christ lived and sacrificed for the church? Yes. The details will be different, of course. Perhaps they won't have to spend an hour or two each evening feeding their wives, cleaning their soiled beds of excrement, trying to help them retain some sense of dignity in the midst of the humiliation they feel as a result of their circumstances. Maybe they won't have to carry their wives out to the car every time they leave the house together. Or they may not have to encourage them to believe that all of those indignities work together for the good, even when they feel completely helpless and undeserving. But the answer is still Yes

If a husband is to live out the implications of the fifth chapter of Ephesians, he ought to commit himself to the relationship with his wife as the primary relationship, aside from his relationship with God, of his life. He ought to understand that the well-being and spiritual development of his wife is the primary commitment of his life. He ought to seek the deepest satisfaction of all human relationships in the marriage relationship, not work-related relationships or other friendships. And he ought to do all of this for the same reason that Jesus gave himself for the sake of his bride: obedience to the Father in heaven.

How did Christ love the church? I mentioned earlier that two things are obvious: He lived for her, and he died for her. What about the "dying" part? How does a husband die for his wife, and should he even think of the relationship like that?

At a surface level, a husband ought always to be willing to die for his wife. He ought to be willing to give his own life if it came down to it, if that giving would save the life of his wife. This was something I thought about in the depths of Debbie's illness, and I came to the place where I was willing to die if it meant that she could have been restored. Of course, there was no real way for such a trade-off to take place, but there were times when I wished for such transference.

At a deeper level, though, I think every husband can and should face the question of dying for the sake of his wife. In the Garden of Gethsemane, the Lord prayed to the Father. He prayed, "If it is possible, let this cup pass from me, yet not as I will, but as you will" (Matthew 26:39). The drinking of the cup was inevitable for the Lord, and it is inevitable for a husband who truly loves his wife. Few husbands will ever have to give their lives physically, taking a mortal blow that their spouse might be saved from death. Those things occasionally happen, say when a man drowns saving his wife from drowning, but those cases are rare. In a spiritual sense, though, husbands must "put to death" their own self-centered desires and ambitions in order to love their wives in the way that Christ loved the church.

Christian men can do this because they have already died in Christ. Paul's letter to the Galatians in 2:19-20 uses the emphatic word crucified. We have been crucified with Christ, and we no longer live, but Christ lives in us. And because we have died in Christ and have also been raised in him (Colossians 3:1-5), we have the power to die to our own concerns and to live for others. Christian men can love their wives as Christ loved the church and not be bitter about making such a sacrifice (Colossians 3:19). We have the power to live in such a way because Christ has given us his resurrection power to equip us for every good act of obedience, and God's Spirit is making us daily into the very image of Christ himself (Colossians 3:9–10). A husband who is being transformed into the image of Christ is being transformed into the image of the one who is united to his bride. That transformation will certainly make a husband a more loving husband.

In both of these areas, Christ's living and dying for his bride, he acted out of obedience to God the Father. Husbands must see that their work of sacrificial love for their wives is more than anything else an act of obedience to God. But such obedience is not drudgery. It may be difficult, but it is not like some dreaded activity that we have to do "just because it is right." It is obedience that brings joy with it. Jesus endured the cross "for the joy set before him" (Hebrews 12:2). That means that Jesus looked beyond the cross for what it would accomplish in the lives of those who would one day be members of his body, the church. Husbands must love their wives for that same joy, for what that love will accomplish in their wives' lives.

There are few joys more profound than a husband's joy as he brings honor and happiness to his wife. It's how God works through the husband on earth. I was learning this truth step by step.

The Face of God on the Face of One Suffering

I still had miles to go before being really able to coast a bit, but I was learning to love—not to fulfill a need of my own, but to follow the sacrificial example of our Savior, and for the pleasure of seeing what my love did for Debbie. This reordering of priorities was profound in itself, but accompanying it was a curious byproduct. I was undergoing a gradual change in my view of the value of human suffering.

One of the biggest spiritual hurdles Christians face when dealing with profound illness or other kinds of suffering is the sense that their problems may be bigger than God. After all, they pray, but don't the sufferings persist? The Jewish people who endured the Holocaust understood that issue very well, and they knew it could go both ways. Richard Rubenstein, a Jewish theologian, became an atheist after the Holocaust. On the other hand, the Jewish intellectual Elie Wiesel experienced a strengthening of his faith in the concentration camp.

How is it that one man lost faith in God and yet another grew in faith while they endured the same basic horror? Wiesel has said that in the concentration camp, he saw the face of God in the faces of the people who were suffering. Debbie and I had been helped earlier by viewing a film about a person in whom we did see the face of God in suffering. That person was Joni Eareckson Tada. I already mentioned one of her many songs that meant so much to us, but I must tell you more about how her life impacted ours.

Joni had had a diving accident in 1967 that left her a quadriplegic for life. (You can read about her journey to faith in her autobiography, *Joni*.) After undergoing two years of rehabilitation, she determined to help others who were facing a life of physical debilitation. In 1979 she founded Joni and Friends (JAF) to accelerate Christian ministry to the disabled. Eventually Joni Eareckson Tada would form the Joni and Friends International Disability Center (IDC) in 2006. We had heard of her even before we turned our lives over to Christ, and eventually we got to meet her.

It is not often that you have the opportunity to come face to face with someone truly great. By any standard, Joni is that kind of person. This is a woman who has faced some of the greatest challenges life can offer, and yet she has more than just survived. A truly great person does more than just overcome problems. A great heart looks away from one's problems and asks how to help others who are also suffering. That describes Joni to the letter.

When we met Joni at a Billy Graham Crusade where she was speaking, her ministry to disabled people was in full gear and we were privileged to begin to develop a friendship with her. We had just become believers, but the influence of this remarkable, caring woman thrust us even more quickly forward into the work of God's Kingdom. The Hound was at our heels, and he was using, among other things, the gentle and compassionate saint Joni Eareckson Tada.

The Christian world needs more people like Joni. One of the most powerful complaints against some Christians is that they may seem to believe that they are right in their convictions, but they don't always demonstrate their faith by their compassion. Convictions are important. In fact, I would say they are crucial. In this postmodern world, where the question of objective truth and one's beliefs don't seem to matter to many people, we need always to be anchored to our convictions about what is true and what is right. Convictions are at the very core of the Christian faith. But conviction without compassion helps no one.

It may be a cliché to express it this way, but it is still true: no one cares how much you know until they know how much you care. Knowledge and caring go hand in hand. The Christian faith is about both Word (objective truth) and Spirit (subjective truth). It is about Scripture and the Work of God, in a practical way, on the human heart. If we abandon the Word in favor of Spirit we lose our backbone; if we abandon Spirit in favor of the Word we lose our hearts. Humans need both backbones and hearts. Without both, we become useless.

Joni has both. While her physical backbone is paralyzed, her spiritual backbone is strong enough to carry others' burdens with lightness and grace. We were greatly encouraged by the opportunity of meeting her and her "friends." The timing was perfect, when we were infants in the faith and just beginning the uncertain path toward our own futures.

But more than anything else, the Lord was also using Debbie in my life and me in hers. Debbie saw the love of Jesus in my love for her, and I saw the grace of God at work in her peacefulness. Debbie and I faced doubts, but we were strengthened by the Lord and we each saw him in one another.

The key to understanding what was going on between us was not in assuming that we were somehow becoming stronger and more capable in and of ourselves. No, it was in glimpsing what God was so capable of doing through us. Said differently, God's desire was for us to be *made usable* for Kingdom purposes. And a significant part of this included the fulfillment of our love for each other *in him*. God does not simply love. He *is Love* personified. He had made Debbie very easy for me to love as he remade her into a person who was so very, very lovable. And of course, if Debbie was lovable to me, how much more was God lovable to me since he himself is the very essence of love!

Being Satisfied With Each Other

Still, these were lonely times, or maybe more accurately, "alone times." This was a real wilderness period in some ways. Although we still were unable go to church meetings regularly, we began to have fellowship with some new Christian friends. This fellowship eventually did lead to our joining a regular church, and to a fellowship that was very important in our spiritual development. But we spent a lot of time together, just the two of us, and we became one flesh—our hearts were melded together during these days. We needed time where it was just Debbie and me and no one else. That brought us solidarity. Over time I seemed to know what she was thinking before she communicated. Of course there were many problems in communication, but the main things I knew. And in a wonderful way I was being rewarded by knowing more deeply some things that other husbands may not have been forced by circumstances to grasp.

We had each other. I am sure many people thought we were reclusive, and in a sense we were. Moving about was just very difficult, not just because Debbie was difficult to move, but also because we feared that moving her too much could create a new medical crisis, something we always dreaded. The motion made her uncomfortable and left her feeling nauseous. This is why we did not go on vacations during most of this early period of time, at least not ones that took us far from home. It was impossible for us to do the kinds of things normal couples did on a routine basis.

In that sense we were not a "normal couple." We were, however, both "sub-normal" and "super-normal." We were below the norm in that we had a severe disability to deal with, and one thing that disabilities do—they disable you! It would have been foolish for us to think that our life together could be just like everyone else's. On the other hand, we saw ourselves as above the norm since we had battled through and survived terrible obstacles. That gave us a bond that would probably have been impossible without our struggle in faith.

It was not easy living mostly alone. Many of our friends did not want to come over and visit with us. They often just did not know how to react to Debbie's condition, and they were afraid they would embarrass themselves or us by their presence. I understood. We abstained even from many family events, though some family members, particularly Debbie's mom, stayed very close to us and made a huge contribution by helping our lives become more manageable. But apart from those few family relationships, we simply did not get very involved with other people. It was simply too difficult. Debbie and I traveled together on our own journey. She loved for me to read books to her. We prayed together almost every day. I would pray on her behalf and record my prayers on tape so she could listen while I was at work. These things enabled us to bond together more and more as the weeks went by.

In the long hours of each day where she sat alone, as a nurse went about her duties, Debbie became a woman of prayer. She would want to "tell" me when I came home in the evenings all of the things she had prayed about, sitting there silently in her chair or on the sofa, engaging in quiet but profound communication with the Lord. I believe that God blessed many, many people through the prayers of this woman confined to her house by her illness, a woman who could not cook a meal or make a bed, but who could pray. She was unable to do anything of a practical nature for herself, her friends or family members. On the other hand, this prayer warrior could do something for others that had much more than merely temporal value. She couldn't crochet a baby blanket or bake a pie, but she could pray for the little one who would be covered at night by the blanket someone else made, and even more with heavenly protection. And she could lift before the Lord those sitting around a table together sharing a meal.

Debbie recognized she would never have become such a praying Christian had it not been for the MS. Her days, probably like the days of most wives, would have been filled with the details of life—cooking, parenting, working, shopping. Instead, she was left with the solitude of her own inner world. She could have withdrawn into that inner life and become depressed, or she could have spent all day every day entertaining herself or in some other way attempting to consume her time with distractions. Of course there was some of that. But Debbie chose to remember her problems and the problems of others, and she took them to the Lord rather than hashing them and rehashing them over and over in her mind.

Psalm 55 was written by David after his son, Absalom, drove him out of Jerusalem. Absalom had taken control of the kingdom in a *coup*, and King David was forced to flee. Sometime later, probably as he sat by a fireside in the wilderness one cool evening, he wrote the lament that became this psalm. In it, David mentions his many struggles and problems and his being attacked from all sides, and he asks for God's help when he declares, "as for me, I will call upon God and the Lord shall save me. Evening and morning and at noon I will pray, and cry aloud, and he shall hear my voice" (Psalm 55:16-17). Interesting. David did not try to forget his problems, but instead, he remembered them before God.

That is what Debbie did. She remembered her problems and the problems of countless other people, and she put them in front of God. In fact, I knew that what brought her the greatest satisfaction was interceding for people and worshipping the Lord. My wife spent long stretches of time almost every day in prayer. If she knew of someone having a problem or an illness, she would pray for that person. When the person she was praying for had some kind of deliverance, Debbie was overjoyed. She had become like a praying centrifuge, casting her prayers all over the world at God's feet from that chair she was sitting in. All the while she watched and took great pleasure in seeing God at work in other peoples' lives, even though there was no evidence that her own condition was improving and no firm reason to believe that it ever would.

What I witnessed in Debbie amazed me and still amazes me. This person one would assume primarily to be the object of other people's prayers (and she was) was also a woman who saw others' difficulties as more important than her own. Within the fading glory of her earthly shell emerged a vivid living testimony of conformity to the image of Christ. *Such precious clay!*

Chapter 7

The Good, the Bad, and the Challenging

⹎

Hurdles and Ironies

AS THE 1980s moved on, we continued dealing with the unrelenting daily challenges. During warfare, battles sometimes result in what military people call "collateral damage." In our case there were obvious collateral problems stemming from Debbie's illness. Such difficulties are not new to people dealing with debilitating physical conditions, but these problems were part and parcel of our experience and therefore an important element of what God was doing in our lives.

One of our most frustrating and enduring challenges was obtaining medical insurance. Imagine this: When Debbie became disabled, because of her inability to work, she was released from her job as a nurse and her medical insurance was duly terminated. After this, I could not obtain coverage for her on my policy because she had what they deemed to be a *pre-existing condition*! The old double-bind. This troubling irony has never left me. It reminds me of the so-called "roofer's guarantee": *When the water runs in, the guarantee runs out.*

Another ongoing challenge was obtaining nursing care. Debbie's condition did not technically require constant medical attention, at least not yet, but we needed to have a nursing care person who would know what to do in dealing with Debbie's disease and who would also know how to handle minor emergencies. Since, for now, her condition was designated as needing only *custodial care*, the insurance would not pay for this even when I was eventually able to obtain coverage for her. Family members helped out in sitting with Debbie as they could, but there was still a great need for health care at home. The only option was for me to pay nurses out of my own pocket.

The aides we hired, the ones I could afford, came with lots of baggage and all kinds of problems. Some of them would talk all day about their own problems, with no consideration for the fact that they were there to help a woman who had far more to be sad about than they did. Though Debbie prayed through the day and tried not to be flustered by these individuals, they would sometimes drive her crazy with things they said. Many were selfish, and some really had no conception about how to minister to a helpless woman. Boy, could I tell some stories!

One aide from the city turned out to have been an ex-prostitute. That in itself would not have been a disqualification; after all, Jesus had a heart for the lowest dregs of society. But she was dishonest and completely incompetent. Only later did I learn of horrible drunken abuses, much too awful to detail. The problem is that you don't often realize how some people are going to work out until you actually hire them and see what happens. Even then, not being on the scene made supervision nearly impossible. Debbie, of course, was unable to react and I think she was fearful about communicating to me what may have happened, suspecting that if I were to confront the problem the aide's abuse might get worse. Each day it seemed a chunk of my heart was ripped out as I had no alternative but to watch the love of my life endure this unspeakable torturous progression. People can do a lot of emotional damage in a matter of a few days or a couple of weeks. It would be a long time before I had real peace about what was going on at home with the nursing help I had to hire.

Then came the hurdle of some other well-meaning Christians. Some of the women from a local church would come to visit on occasion. These women started telling me things I could not quite grasp at first. They informed me that I was the roadblock to Debbie's healing. I was somewhat theologically naïve at the time, but I eventually figured out that they held to an extreme form of the Christian faith teaching that anyone with any unhealed illness is simply not believing God for their healing. In other words, they believe that every illness, without exception, will yield to a prayer of faith. If one is not being healed, there is obviously not enough faith. These women and this unbiblical doctrine wrought havoc in my home for a number of weeks.

I know there are many godly and wonderful people who have strong views about physical healing. They love the Lord, believe the Bible, and for the most part do not hold the extreme views being taught by the ladies who were visiting Debbie. I might have some differences of biblical interpretation with good people who believe in and practice healing, yet I would not disagree with them on the major issues of the Christian faith. But these movements do have their fringe members, as is true for many other charismatic as well as non-charismatic groups, and the women who were coming to my house were definitely part of that wildly foolish and dangerous fringe. I eventually had to ask them not to come to our home any longer.

The irony here is that some people think they are taking the Bible very seriously when they are actually not taking it seriously enough. Even as a new Christian I recognized that. God never promises to heal us of every sickness in this life, and even some of the godliest people in the Bible were ill to the point of death. The apostle Paul had what he described as a suffering, or a "thorn in the flesh," which many biblical scholars interpret as a physical ailment (2 Corinthians 12:7–10). He also instructed Timothy to drink wine for his stomach troubles and the other ailments he seemed frequently to have (1 Timothy 5:23). Paul did not simply command the illnesses to leave and "claim" healing, but rather he dealt with the problems in other ways. Faith is important, and we should never forget to pray for our healing and the healing of others. But we also need to recognize that some healings only occur in the age to come.

To make matters worse, the aide—the same one I described earlier— also told these women I was having an affair with her. That charge, if not so sad and hurtful, would have been humorous. That is not to say I hadn't been tempted at times in that way. Wouldn't any man in my spot have had to deal with temptation? But I had certainly never been tempted when I thought of her!

But those false accusations were only a small part of the problem. I had not yet put all the hints together, but slowly it became evident that this nurse was an evil woman. I knew Debbie was vulnerable and that she could not deal with the issues. She would sometimes endure bad things happening to her and not "tell" me until later, since she knew she had no other alternative than to put up with the treatment when I was not there. I have never been able to understand how any person could take advantage of someone this helpless in any way whatsoever. I had plenty of reminders of the presence of sin in this world as I tried to find nurses who could be trusted.

Caring for Debbie was a difficult matter; her mother and I did it out of love, but for those who did not love her, there often wasn't enough pay to convince them that this was a worthwhile task. This was also very frustrating for Debbie. At one level she understood, but at another level she wondered why it was so difficult for people to do the work they had agreed to do when they were hired. Did they just not want the responsibility? Were they frightened or intimidated? Did they see Debbie's condition as a tragedy they were not emotionally or spiritually equipped to handle?

Collateral Damages

"Small potatoes," you may recall Debbie used to say, when she was still able to talk. Yet we both realized how difficult it must have been for them to see a young woman ravaged by the physical damages of MS. She had been helplessly observing these reactions since she first began to lose motor functions and the ability to manage her personal hygiene needs, and since her features had begun to deteriorate due to her malady.

Debbie typically needed a cloth to be placed below her mouth to absorb the saliva that ran down her chin. At times her eyes were stuck in a stare, as she was unable to consistently control her facial expressions. Her once cared-for hair now at best had the "nurse-of-the-day do," not exactly what a pretty young wife had in mind. The steroid medications and other treatments we tried—and we tried a variety both approved and experimental, from prescribed medications to herbs to homeopathic remedies—would sometimes leave her with profuse acne and puffy weight gain.

Her muscles got very tense. Her legs calcified at the knee joints, and doctors at one point considered cutting the ligaments to allow them to straighten. Her fingers were also contracted so badly that we had to put towel rolls in her hands to prevent her nails from digging into her palms.

Yet, often after an agonizing spasm she would smile and sometimes even laugh after the residual pain wore off. What a sport! But even laughing was dangerous for Debbie, though. She might get started and laugh so hard that her nostrils would flair and then she would begin to struggle with her breathing.

Not surprisingly, perhaps, Debbie sometimes thought of herself as a burden. I guess it's not hard to understand why someone would not enjoy having to clean up soiled bed sheets and even do digital lubrication to help her to have bowel movements. It got to the point that when interviewing someone, I would first explain "the case" to them as they would view her in our room through separating French doors. This would spare Debbie yet one more rejection, or worse, uncaring and even abusive treatment by her caregivers. I could cry, and I did. I probably did not cry often enough, in light of the way my wife was sometimes made to feel.

Regardless of her drastically altered physical appearance, Debbie's inner glow was often evident. She was like a window through which God's light was shining brightly. But not everyone took the time to look. Those who did take the time found their efforts richly rewarded by the ministry of love and faith that came to them from her.

Watching my love suffer so deeply broke my hardened heart piece by piece. Somehow I was being softened and hardened at the same time. I was softened with compassion for my beloved lady and at the same time hardened with an ever-increasing hatred for the sin that was so pervasive in this cursed, unrighteous world (Romans 1:18). To this day I confess it still angers me when I think of that struggle to find adequate and compassionate caregivers. In a way my anger may have been a limited human replica of God's own righteous anger over the sin that is so destructive in this world.

So one year went by and then two. Now it seemed I was strong enough in the Lord to be able to stand on the truth as I knew it to be. I had come a long way in a couple of years. Debbie and I began to connect in ways I would have never dreamed before. I have to admit that I was still quite selfish, but increasingly the depth of my selfishness was being revealed to me little by little. I began to understand how Christ crucified our flesh on the cross, but we still have to "live by the Spirit" to avoid carrying out the desire of the sinful flesh (Galatians 5:16).

I probably spent more time *working* during this early period than I should have. The Lord still had much to teach me about what it means to rest in him and love my wife as Christ loved the church. I was not as far along as I wanted to be, but thankfully I was farther along than I had been only a year or two earlier.

A Good Dream Coming True

Can you think of a particular time in your life when you had a dream you really hoped would come true? And even though there were all kinds of obstacles, it did come true! Then as things turned out, this became one of your great success stories. Or maybe you had a dream that just fizzled out and went away, a dream unfulfilled. How did you cope with that situation? Were you intimidated by the turn of events?

Were you afraid this failure might just be the one that derails you for the rest of your life? Did you lose confidence, wondering whether you could believe in yourself any more, or whether those who were close to you could still believe in you?

I've certainly had my share of failures. But I think there is something about the way God wired me that enabled me somehow, by his grace, to design and build beautiful things. I love to build and see things happen when I apply myself to the challenge of creating and constructing something new. Even before I was in high school a friend and I were cutting trees down in the woods and building a little one-room cabin. That in itself was a kind of dream that came true, albeit a much smaller dream than the ones that came later.

I gained quite a bit of experience through high school doing construction work. I had a knack for it and really enjoyed it. A major life's dream for me was to design and build my own house. As you may remember, not long after we married Debbie and I had a lot of dreams, but they no longer seemed possible as she became so very ill. But I was not going to let go of this one. Maybe it was my ego or even selfishness, but I prayed that God would give me the desire of my heart, the desire to build the home I'd always wanted for Debbie.

We actually ended up *needing* to move. The stairs of our little three-story carriage house were now nearly impossible to navigate and becoming more so each day. God began to answer our prayer and allow us our "dream home." It would be away from the noise of the town, a place of solitude where our ears would be filled with only the soothing sounds of nature. Though we loved the carriage house we knew that we needed to take the difficult step of leaving it behind. In a relatively small way we were each beginning to learn one of the lessons regarding the seasons of life that would only become more significant. Often it seems that to dream again we must be willing to leave something cherished behind. And so we did.

So I spoke to my mother-in-law, asking her if she'd be willing to commit to a year to help care for my wife, her daughter. This was the first of many obstacles we would have to face in order to make this happen. She agreed. God then led me to a piece of property that a man in Texas had owned and hadn't been able to sell for years. But as I saw it on the multiple listing at a price that looked too good to be true, I took a drive by and saw why it nearly was too good to be true.

First of all there was a twenty foot rock ridge blocking access to five and a half of the six acres. But that wasn't the only obstacle. I climbed over the ridge to find a junkyard staring me in the face. (It seems that back at the turn-of-the-century the community was using this area as a landfill or dump.) I offered the owner $11,000, which was half his asking price for six acres. I wrote him a long letter explaining why it was only worth that much. He agreed, and I bought the property. I then spent $5,000 to blast through the ridge and then spent weeks moving old cars, hundreds of tires, windshields, car seats, and every other thing imaginable. I moved them off to a place where I was able to bury them with blasted rock from the ridge.

I was also able to construct a beautifully winding driveway to the back of the property, using a wonderful base of blasted rock. The project to build our dream home began, but I ran into obstacle after obstacle, including finances. Just as I began laying the concrete blocks for the foundation of our dream house, the company I was working for suddenly decided they were going to dissolve our division. The position I was then offered was not in line with my career goals. Effectively, I was out of a job.

But God gave me focus and perseverance. I had a sort of creative euphoria during the weeks between the old job and a new one. I camped out under the stars. I would rinse myself off in the stream in the morning and get back to work. For many years afterwards Debbie and I enjoyed that home in the woods as our special retreat, our dream come true.

Chapter 8

Turning up the Heat

Lessons from the Kitchen

YOU HAVE TO eat in order to live. That is pretty obvious, and eating is something most of us take for granted. We just reach into the refrigerator, grab a morsel and pop it into our mouths. Nothing could be simpler. In fact, the simplicity of this act is what has resulted in many people eating more than they should and thus creating a new complexity where none existed before—how to stop from eating everything we feel inclined to grab from the refrigerator and pop into our mouths. But in this area, as in so many others I have discussed already, eating was not simple in our home, and it became less and less so as time went by.

Scripture has much to say about eating. It actually begins with the Lord making the man and woman and telling them what they could and could not eat. As we all know, they decided they wanted to make their own decision about that, thank you very much. The results were not good. We also find that when the Israelites were wandering in the wilderness, God prepared a table for them in the desert and provided food for forty years.

Just before his betrayal, arrest and trial, Jesus sat down and shared a meal with his closest followers, his disciples, something we refer to as the Last Supper. Later, in the book of Revelation, Jesus gives a message to John the apostle, telling him "behold, I stand at the door and knock.

If anyone hears my voice and opens the door, I will come in to him and dine with him, and he with me" (Revelation 3:20). At the very end of this age there will be a great feast, the marriage supper of the Lamb, as God celebrates his final victory over evil (Revelation 19). So, meals are important, even important in spiritual ways and not only for sustaining our physical bodies.

Though Debbie loved to prepare meals before her illness, she very soon became incapable of doing so. Her hands trembled when she tried to handle the cookware or to measure out ingredients. She dropped food on the floor. She soon realized it was dangerous for her to try continuing to cook. Cooking became one more thing she had to "die" to, along with dressing herself and applying make-up. Over time, she also had to give up many of her favorite foods, especially as she lost the ability to chew and swallow effectively. This was a major part of the process of descending into the pit of helplessness that accompanied her disease.

I learned how to cook and serve meals early in Debbie's illness. I also developed skill in feeding her. This was sometimes a long and frustrating process, since her motor skills were growing worse all the time. Sometimes neighbors would also bring food for us to eat. Her food had to be converted to a liquid paste since feeding her anything solid risked causing her to choke, which could lead to severe pulmonary issues and even to her death.

Feeding Debbie was something akin to feeding very small babies. Every mother who has fed an infant knows what it is like when the baby is first old enough to start taking something besides mother's milk or formula. The child can now handle something besides mere liquid, but not much more than that. So the mother meticulously makes sure that any solids are extremely tiny in order to prevent the possibility that they might become lodged in the baby's throat.

It is amazing what God can teach you in the kitchen. You may have heard of Brother Lawrence, the simple Carmelite monk who wrote the classic, *The Practice of the Presence of God*. Lawrence was required to perform the practical and mundane duties that all in the monastery shared, such as kitchen duties. He particularly disliked this task, but he learned that work done unto God can make his presence as real in simple duties, such as washing dishes, as it is in prayer.

I did not particularly dislike the task of preparing food, feeding Debbie, and then cleaning up afterward. But I did find it to be a real challenge to my patience. I prefer to move from task to task, accomplishing things as quickly as possible, and then move on to the next project. Feeding Debbie, though, might take as long as an hour for each meal.

Had I not been taught by Scripture about the most important issues in life, I might very well have found myself being increasingly resentful of the process. It is easy to be hardened by infirmity, to sense that one is merely a victim of circumstances. People often blame God in such matters, even if they don't think much about God in any other kind of way. There is a saying often repeated by people with disabilities and by those who minister to them: "We can either get bitter or better." It is easy to be hardened—that is the world's response to suffering. But to be softened by such events—that is God's way.

It is important to learn the importance of priorities. Earning a living is important. Living in what is sometimes the fast pace of life in the business world can be an important part of one's daily routine. Sometimes people complain about work and the hours spent "making a living." But we must always recognize the blessing and value of work. It not only provides food and shelter for our families, but it often offers fulfillment and satisfaction to the one working.

No less important is providing physical, emotional, and spiritual care for those we love and who depend on us. Often caring for someone requires a different pace of living from that of the workplace. And you can only live at that different pace if you have a different perspective on what is important.

Many men need to learn this lesson more than women do. Most of the women I've observed seem to have better skills in tailoring the pace to the need than men do. Often men want to live their lives at one pace and one pace only, the pace that best suits their own personalities. This, however, is not the way life is. The engine driving a man's life needs multiple speed settings, one speed at work, another with his wife, another with his children, another in his relationship to God, and so on. If he handles everything with the same speed setting, he is going to have a very difficult time being successful in the various areas of life.

Failure to adjust one's speed to the need lies at the root of the struggle many men have in developing satisfaction in every sphere. They may be very successful at work, but perhaps their wives are unfulfilled or their children are resentful. Or, on the other hand, a man might have a great relationship with his family, but be incapable of providing an adequate living. Every sphere of life is important, but to make it all work together with the right kind of panache one has to find a way of living at different speeds. This was the kind of lesson I learned in the kitchen while feeding Debbie.

I also learned many others. God was teaching me patience, and I can say from experience that spiritual lessons generally are not learned once and for all, never again in need of reinforcement. We are sinful creatures, even as believers, and we need to be taught some lessons more than once. Educators say the key to learning is repetition. If that is so, then God, the Master Teacher, was making sure I learned these lessons on patience so well I would never forget them.

Eating to Live

By 1987 Debbie was having more and more of a difficult time swallowing her food. Furthermore, on days when she was especially ill, feeding was becoming almost impossible. Choking became more and more a matter of concern for us. We knew that before long we would have to figure out how to continue feeding my precious Beeba. She would struggle to swallow and begin to drool, and then she would often begin to cough in gasping coughs accompanied by deep and uncontrollable stiffening. This would result in her being extremely weary, sometimes to the point that she was too exhausted to take another bite. It was heart-wrenching to see her cough and drool in that manner.

The fear of choking brought on a further fear—another emergency trip to the hospital. As you now know, Debbie feared hospitals almost as much as she feared anything. Neither she nor I thought hospitals and their employees were usually incompetent. We knew better than that. Most of the doctors, nurses and other health care professionals at our nation's hospitals are quite competent. We had just had too many bad experiences, and when hospital personnel deal with someone whose medical situation is very complex, there is always a greater possibility that something will go wrong. We both knew this, and we both wanted to avoid such an eventuality as much as we possibly could.

Her doctors recommended that we have a gastrostomy tube, what most people call a "feeding tube," installed so that during days when it was hard for her to swallow she would still be able to receive nourishment. They also informed me that as time went by, it was likely she would lose much of her ability to take food orally and that the gastrostomy tube would become the primary means of administering food to her. Because of all that, they said, it was now time for us to decide if we wanted to authorize this procedure.

There are different types of gastrointestinal feeding devices. Some are introduced through the nose or the mouth. These are generally only used in situations where such a feeding device will only be needed for a short period of time. Debbie's situation was quite different, since she was likely to need this tube for the rest of her life. The type of device she required is essentially a piece of tubing penetrating through the lower part of one's abdomen. This requires a surgical procedure, as the doctors make an incision in the skin, then puncture the stomach wall and insert the device directly into the stomach from the front of the abdomen.

Agreeing to this operation was a major decision for us. It meant that my beautiful wife was now going to have her body invaded by another permanent piece of equipment. She previously had reluctantly agreed to a urinary catheter for the convenience of her caregivers. We had many questions about the prescribed surgery, and our doctors did the best they could to convey that this was an essential procedure for Debbie's ability to eat—and without being able to eat she would not survive.

Though her communication skills were severely altered by her deteriorating condition, Debbie was able to make it clear that she hated this prospect. It had been dehumanizing enough for her to endure the ravages of the disease. Yes, she was very ill, but she had not lost her self-respect nor her desire to look as good as she possibly could. As I talked with her about this need to have the tube placed, I saw in her eyes the pain it was causing her just to think about this. One more step of submission to a terrifying future. One more way in which this illness was transforming her into something she did not like. It broke my heart. She despised the thought of it, but she made it clear she was leaving the decision to me.

I gave my consent to installing the tube, not fully realizing what we were in for. Nonessential people are usually not allowed in the operating room during a surgical procedure, but I convinced the doctors to allow me to be with her. It was a good thing I was there, but I was not prepared for the terrible trauma to follow. After securing her head and restraining her jaws with blocks between her teeth so they would not close, they ran a tube down her esophagus with a light at the end. Then they pushed the light all the way into her stomach, and then dimmed lights in the room so they could see through her skin and know where to make the incision for the tube. Debbie began to endure great discomfort as the tube went down. She was on the verge of panic, and only my presence in the room kept her from major emotional trauma. As her neck tightened and her muscles contracted involuntarily things got worse. Her jaws began to cramp and she began having spasms against the blocks between her molars. Never before had I heard such powerful wails of human suffering. No one in the room was prepared for this.

This was a new low, one of the worst moments of our entire ordeal up to that point. I found it very difficult to fight off the emotions raging in my heart—anger at the doctors, fear of what might happen to Debbie, and frustration at my inability to do anything about it. Her willing response to the choice I made for her to undergo this procedure remains to this day a vivid picture of her submission to me as her "head" under God (1 Corinthians 11:3). I find myself thinking of Christ, who submitted willingly to unbearable agony to fulfill his task of redeeming humankind.

Debbie's agony will forever be etched in my memory. And yet the testimony of our love for each other became evident to everyone around. As I coached and prayed her through the pain, everyone in the room noticed this was no mere normal "pep talk" kind of coaching. I am confident it was also obvious to the "rulers and authorities in the heavenly realms" (Ephesians 3:10). That is the apostle Paul's way of saying that even unseen spiritual forces in the universe observe God's people in their times of trial. I just came to Debbie's side and told her, "Look to Jesus. Just look to Jesus. He will help you through this moment." Ultimately her body's involuntary struggle seemed to subside and the doctors were able to complete the procedure.

"With Wings like Eagles"

I had recently been reading the Old Testament book of Job. I felt more and more like the Bible character Job than I ever had. He, of course, experienced the loss of virtually everything in his life. At the end of many trials Job developed a greater appreciation for the person, power, and presence of God in his life than he had ever known before his troubles. I recalled the New Testament story of the Prodigal Son. The father in that account allowed his son to leave home and go into a far country, knowing that this was the only way for the son truly to understand his lostness.

At this terrible moment, Debbie and I were becoming more aware all of the time of our deep need for fellowship with God. Like Job, I felt that I had all I dreamed of and more, yet I needed to need God, and that need was being developed through our horrible medical ordeal. When one is rich, it is easy to mask the needs in one's heart by replacing that need with material things and exciting experiences. And of course, "rich" is relative. One does not have to own the wealth of someone like Job (and he was extremely wealthy) to hide the need from oneself for God. Rich, poor, or somewhere in between, we are masters at masking or burying the need in multiple ways. Finding God had made our experience very different. In other words, suffering was driving us toward God, not away from him. So really, it wasn't a question of us finding God so much as it was of God pursuing us.

Scripture teaches that suffering reminds us we are made for a greater world than this one. Paul wrote, "The sufferings of this present time are not worthy to be compared to the glory which shall be revealed in us" (Romans 8:18). The apostle then discusses what will happen at the second coming of Jesus Christ. It is easy for many people simply to be completely satisfied with this age, with the material things of life, and with the nature of relationships as we experience them now. But the experience of suffering causes one to look beyond and to ask the simple question, "Is this the best it will ever be?" The Bible says no, absolutely not.

Some readers might be inclined to say, "Oh, then, what you are really saying is you could not cope with your difficulties, and so you turned to religion as a crutch to help you out. Are you not afraid this is all just 'pie in the sky?'" Those are fair comments, but they emphatically do not reflect our experience. Remember that I was resistant to the idea of faith from the very beginning. I was an agnostic, and maybe even a borderline atheist. I wanted to be a self-made man. I believed then, and I still believe today, in standing up and working hard and taking what life gives you "like a man."

We did not turn to God merely because we were suffering. We turned to God because we became convinced that Jesus is the Son of God, that he died for our sins, and that he is worthy of following. And it was God himself who convinced us of our need as he drew us in through Debbie's suffering. Some tragedies are so profound they are never completely healed in the seen world; they must wait until the unseen age to come. All of this world's ills will never be finally resolved in this period, but only in the millennium on Earth or everlastingly in heaven, where there will be complete harmony in all of God's creation. Believing this does not represent an escapist diversion of the mind from unpleasant realities to imagined bliss. Christian teaching emphasizes the importance of facing our problems straight on, but facing them trusting God for strength for the day. That is not an attempt to escape or to pretend that things are just fine when they are not. Believe me, our life together represented anything but escapism.

What Debbie and I discovered, and Debbie was discovering it more profoundly than me at the time, was that thinking of the glory to come made her difficulties bearable. She would go through a choking spell, or deal with a fever, or suffer through one of the many days of distress that were part of our life together during these middle years of coping with the disease. But whereas she might expect to drift into despair over these things, her reaction was quite the opposite. She dealt with her pain and discomfort, recognizing that this was just the prelude to something better.

We are foreigners and strangers in this world (1 Peter 2:11). As pilgrims, there is a very real sense that we were made for another world, not this one. To put it simply, we don't belong here, and we wait in expectation of something far better. This is a complex idea and it is not easily explainable. In one sense, we do belong here because this is the world God has made. He created it for humans made in the divine image to represent him in this age and on this earth. But the rebellion of his creatures caused this world to fall from its original perfection. Not only are humans fallen, but the physical world itself exists in a fallen condition, and even the world itself longs for release from this terrible state of affairs (Romans 8:22). We groan in these fallen, physical bodies, and the world around us, including the trees, the grass, the hills, the very stars in the heavens, groan with us, like a woman about to give birth, longing for the day when universal decay will come to a screeching halt. When one realizes there will always be the taint of sorrow and the blight of death on this age, one comes to know the ultimate solution is found not here in this world, but elsewhere in the approaching world to come. Debbie understood this.

I would walk into the room where she was lying. I knew she'd had a coughing fit, or that she was struggling with fever. But her face was glowing; it was not twisted with the struggle to keep emotional control, but was almost supernaturally content. Sometimes after a dangerous episode, she would begin to laugh uncontrollably. Debbie's laughter was a heavenly melody to me, a song from her heart as she faced the unending drag of the illness on her body.

Isaiah 40:31 became a favorite verse for us: "Those who wait on the Lord. . . shall mount up with wings like eagles." Physically, Debbie was not mounting up anywhere. But in her heart, I believe she was soaring higher than any eagle has ever flown. She was looking at our world and its decay not from a vantage point within that world, but from above, where she was seated with Christ in heavenly realms (Ephesians 2:4–6). An eagle overcomes the law of gravity by a higher law, the physics of flight—velocity plus lift. Debbie was also overcoming the law of physical decay by a higher law, the law of faith and trust in God. His purposes are better and higher than ours, even when we are at a loss completely to understand them.

Some will wonder why, if our faith was so real, there was not enough faith to believe God for Debbie's healing. Anyone undergoing the kind of trauma we endured all those years thinks a lot about healing. A lot! Healing becomes a daily matter of prayer. And for couples like Debbie and me, whose very marriage was almost defined by the ordeal they faced together, healing is not simply a theoretical or theological matter (though it is theological as well). The question of healing is something you confront literally every day of your life. You pray for healing in all kinds of ways: "Lord, please heal my wife." "Lord, if it be your will, please restore Debbie to her full strength and health." "Lord, please grant us the grace of healing." "Lord, we claim Debbie's healing in Your Name." You pray and pray for it, at least I did.

Seven and then eight years into the illness I was still constantly praying those same prayers. Ten years into the illness I still believed God had the power to heal my wife if he chose to do so. But in Bible study, in theological reflection, in the intersection between our faith and the reality of what was going on in our life together, we also knew that God did not heal everyone who asked for it. I was convinced that if anyone deserved to be healed, simply due to the strength of her faith and godliness, it was my beloved Debbie. But as the years rolled on, healing did not come. Quite the opposite. Debbie became sicker and sicker.

We never really gave up hope for healing. But we also recognized that if this condition was not God's will, then we had to find out how to walk and live within his plan in the context of our suffering. We realized that future hope enabled us to endure the present struggles, and we knew healing was a certainty for Debbie. The only question was whether it would be in this life or the next one. And in addition to that, we came to understand that sometimes it is only within the orbit of terrible pain and difficulty that God can become so incredibly real.

Author John Newport calls this the revelational principle of suffering. By this he means that encountering physical evil and suffering can become the occasion of our entry into the fuller knowledge of the Lord. In the Old Testament, Hosea's experience of domestic sorrow prepared him to deliver the prophetic message God wanted for him to give, and though his suffering was of a different nature than ours, it nonetheless led him to know God more fully. Paul makes a similar point in the eighth chapter of Romans. When he says God causes all things to work together for good to those who love the Lord (8:28), the "all things" refers to what Paul has just been talking about in the previous verses, that is, suffering. He then promises us that none of this can separate us from the love of God, and he says it in such a way that it is clear this type of suffering, far from removing us from God, far from making God an unknown figure of gloom and doom, actually makes the Creator more palpable and real.

Let me state clearly what was happening. As our suffering together became more and more intense over the years, the reality of God's person and presence became more and more intense, as well. It was as if God's personal care and presence became a kind of mirror of the illness itself. Or perhaps a better image is that God was like the sparring partner of the sickness. As the disease began to deliver heavier and heavier blows, the Lord was able to take the blows on our behalf and to enable us to endure. Even more than endure. The apostle Paul says that we are "more than conquerors" through our Lord (Romans 8:35–39). There is nothing in all of creation that can separate us from God's love. Not life. Not death. Not angels. Not spirits. Not even the present or the future or powers above or below can separate us from the love of God. We came to experience that confidence in a real and substantial way in the midst of a desperate situation. As a deep sea diver has to put on a pressurized suit in order to cope with the extreme conditions of life far below the surface, so we found that, if we clothed ourselves in Christ, we were more than ready to cope with the other overwhelming pressures of our daily lives.

It was absolutely amazing. In the early years of dealing with Debbie's disease, we were often discouraged by even small difficulties, such as the problems with communication I have mentioned. But as time went by, we found ourselves dealing with much more difficult issues, and doing so without nearly as much anxiety and frustration as we had felt in dealing with those smaller matters. This was not just because we had learned some skills, though we had done that. It was because God was more and more real to us all the time. I am thoroughly convinced that people who endure great tribulations can have knowledge of God that is far more intense than others whose lives have been filled with nothing but good things. Jewish philosopher Martin Buber said that "the human spirit can endure anything except perpetual prosperity." These words now have enriched meaning deep within my soul.

Even as the Hebrew boys in the book of Daniel were brought to the place of recognizing the Son of God in the fiery furnace, similarly, we had been made aware of the very person of the Lord himself in the depths of our own ordeal of fire. Because of how pain and suffering can make us grow in our faith, I encourage people all the time not to ask for them, but at the same time not to fear them when they do come. We must realize that for all of us, at some point in the process of life, suffering will come our way. It can't be dodged. When it comes, we should not flee from it, if for no other reason than that God will become real to us in the ordeal in ways we've never imagined before.

As for Debbie and me, the fire of God's love burned in our hearts, bringing warmth to our hardened areas, illuminating those parts of our lives still darkened by our natural, human tendencies. He gave light to us step by step along the way, enabling us to know his ways even better. As we learned to look to the Lord, we found that he enabled us to master the lurking giants of hopelessness, the joy stealers, the kind of self pity that comes from Satan, the encroaching death sentence that always clamors for our attention. The brilliant resurrection life of Christ was burning in us quietly but intensely, and it was ever burning away the dross of our sin, burning ever more brightly all the time.

Our joy increased as we identified with and invested our time and very lives in others who were also facing the kind of decay and brokenness we were enduring. We became friends with other people who faced terminal illness, or various forms of physical handicap and debilitation. These were fellow pilgrims on earth, looking for a country of their own, as the writer of Hebrews put it (11:13-14). Like Debbie and me, they were looking for that place where there will be no more need for sun, moon, or stars, because God himself will be their Everlasting Light. His glory will radiate to all who see that sight, causing us to fall prostrate in worship, in speechless wonder at the greatness of our Redeemer. But those who engage in that act of worship will no longer be broken jars of clay; rather, they will be glorified with the same glory that God himself possesses. As Paul said, we will then be without spot or wrinkle

(Ephesians 5:27), and we will radiate the unfathomable all-surpassing Glorious One who is our Savior.

These fellow children of God, these earthen vessels, though they had previously been broken and even returned to the dust of the earth from which they were first created, are now completely renewed by the glorious Master Potter. They no longer dwell in the shadow lands of the former age, but they now see face to face the One who set love and affection on them.

Isn't that what the Christian life is supposed to be about? Knowing God? And one day knowing the Lord face to face in an unmediated experience of his presence and power? I believe that it is. If that is what the Christian life is all about, we should not ultimately fear the paths that lead us to that knowledge.

I pray that the God of Hope will fill my readers with happiness and peace as you trust in him through the challenges and sufferings that come with this present age. I also pray you will be inundated with the kind of hope coming to us through the inner work of the Holy Spirit (Romans 15:13).

Chapter 9

From Pain to Crisis

—⟨⟨⟨⊙

A Critical Situation

BACK TO THE account of that day when the feeding tube was first put in place. It had not been an easy procedure, but it was done, and it seemed as though Debbie and I would now be able to handle feeding issues more easily than in the past. Whenever she was feeling up to the challenge we would still try to feed Debbie by mouth—mush, of course, but even so, it was so much more pleasant for her to taste her food on her tongue, and she had so few earthly pleasures still available for her to enjoy. We continued to do so for a long time after the tube was installed. She loved to just taste the foods, even when at times she was unable to swallow them. But with the tube in place, we now had options at those times when regular feeding was difficult, and we also had the way to continue feeding her in the event she would no longer be able to take food by mouth.

When we went home, everything seemed fine—at first. But late in the evening, after using the new gastrostomy tube for the first time, Debbie suddenly became very ill. I called the doctor, hoping he would tell me it was not a serious matter and that we would not have to return to the hospital. Instead, he urged me to bring her back to the hospital immediately. It became clear that she could soon die! I drove so fast that a policeman pulled me over, but when he saw her he soon realized how urgent the situation was. Without pause he ushered us down the highway with an emergency escort.

Several doctors were waiting there when we arrived, and they rushed her in for an examination. After brief deliberation they determined the tube had been inserted incorrectly and that her entire peritoneal cavity was contaminated. The food was going to the wrong place! Debbie's fever spiked and she began to lose consciousness. They prepped her for surgery, fearful she would not survive without a respirator. The surgeons had to cut open her torso and expose her vital organs in a mad dash to decontaminate her system before the infection would kill her. Debbie's condition was critical and I would not know for some days whether she would survive the effort of her physicians to give her another chance at life.

I'll never forget my first glimpse of my wife that night after the surgery. I paced back and forth for a few hours while she was in recovery. Finally I was able to enter the recovery room.

There was an eerie stillness. Complex medical paraphernalia were transmitting sure but steady beeps. One could sense an intensity and expectancy in the air as those few dear souls connected to the technological support systems panted for life with the help of the only thing connecting them to it.

My heart sank. As I approached my dear bride, she looked like an eighty-year-old woman. I could not believe my eyes. What does this mean? How could she have aged so much in so short a time? What have they done to her?

I barely gained my composure and began to slowly approach her. "Oh my. Oh my." (Actually, my words may have been a bit more colorful.) I proceeded further, closer and closer. As I wiped the tears from my eyes I realized something. She really did look like an old woman! But she was not Debbie. Wrong bed!

Days of Agony and Hope

In spite of the ways God helped us grow through the whole process of Debbie's condition and our situation as a couple, here we were again in a desperate gamble to save her life. This was caused partly by the failure of medical personnel and technology to live up to its promises. I was discouraged. This was like adding insult to injury. It wasn't bad enough that we had to put the wretched feeding tube in her body in the first place, but now this very lifeline became a major threat to her life. How could God expect us to take any more? I told Debbie I was sorry I made the decision that caused her such distress. My heart was broken. The days stretched out seemingly endlessly. Debbie's lungs filled with fluid. Her fever would break, and then return, then it would break and return again. I believed God could help my wife overcome the worst of the disease, but I was not sure how he was going to override the failures of the medical team whose job it was to help her get better.

During those agonizing days, two things became obvious. One was that I could not help but see this crisis as our crisis—not merely hers. God increased my determination to stand with Debbie and remain at her side, cheering her on, urging her to hang in there, and telling her that things were going to be better.

We had already learned we were one flesh in Christ as husband and wife, and the Lord filled me with a passion to coach her through this dark hour. "We are going to make it. You are going to make it. Stand up against this infection and fight it with all your heart." I also fought against discouragement, but for her sake I was filled with a special gift from the Lord to help her remain courageous in the evil day. Like two young trees growing in soil together, this storm caused us to sink our roots of faith deeper in the rich soil of our loving God who met us day by day in the medical mistakes, infections and pain.

The second thing that became obvious was that Debbie continued growing ever stronger in her faith. And this was true even in the days when it appeared she was growing weaker in body. As the Scripture teaches us, though our earthly tent is torn down, we are also being renewed inwardly day by day (2 Corinthians 5; Romans 6). As her body decreased, her spirit increased. She had a gentle peacefulness about her that was obvious to anyone who came into the room. Once a chaplain stopped by to see Debbie, and he told me that when he left her room he knew that he had been ministered to more than he had ministered. The doctors and nurses witnessed this as well, and though not all of them interpreted it as the peace of God controlling her heart, they all said this was a remarkable woman with an amazing resource. As for Debbie, she made it clear in her limited way that she did not blame them for the situation. She was not angry with anyone. Instead she showed only kindness and confidence in her demeanor.

As the Master Potter allowed us to endure the difficulty that came with the loss of a normal eating routine, and as we experienced the breaking process that can occur when surgical procedures do not go smoothly, we were given the incredible opportunity to love those around us. The brilliant light of the Lord shone in spite of the brokenness, giving onlookers a glimpse of the character of Christ within.

As I look back, I'm still perplexed why this procedure was so botched up. But ultimately we rested our hurt and anger and trusted in knowing that God is good and his ways are higher than our ways. His thoughts are higher than our thoughts, even when egregious and preventable mistakes are made.

Eventually Debbie's condition improved. I found myself smiling as time went by. We would blend up her "go-go juice," as we called it, full of nutritious greens and tortellini, or part of a burger. Her tongue would bob in and out as we placed some of the good stuff in her mouth. How she loved her ice cream! No sense dumping *that* down the tube! Her face would beam as she had the chance once again to know the simple pleasure of tasting food. One such occasion took place during this period at Spruce Lake in Pennsylvania at one of the frequent retreats sponsored by the Joni and Friends organization. Our friend Joni Eareckson Tada sang about a "little taste of heaven" and Debbie actually got to taste something at that retreat that surely was heavenly to her.

As days turned to weeks, slowly but surely Debbie's health began to improve. Her lungs drained, and her fever began to abate. It took months for the danger to completely pass, but finally it looked as though we had turned a corner, and the Lord had proven again it was not time for my bride to leave this world. More than that, God empowered us to face even the worst kind of crisis—a very real and very present mortal crisis—and helped us face it with the kind of confidence that others could not help but notice.

Eventually, we could even see some humor in those scary days. A few months later when I told Debbie about mistaking her for the eighty-year-old woman in another bed, she laughed hysterically, nostrils flaring and even gasping to breathe!

"That the Work of God Might Be Displayed. . ."

One of the most important things we learned in those difficult days was that no event in life is meaningless. As an example, when something goes wrong, say when a doctor makes an injurious incision or fails to make a proper stitch in closing a cut, many seem to chalk this up to just plain bad luck—one of those silly and uncontrollable events in life that cannot be explained. That is not what I believe.

I say there is no such thing as just "bad luck" in the way people normally use that terminology. There is absolutely no meaningless event in life. I know of course that such a belief will seem strange to many people in our world today. A soldier in a battle has a shell fragment whisk past his ear, just missing him and allowing him to live. In the next instant that same fragment strikes his best friend in the carotid artery, and in minutes, before help can arrive, his friend bleeds to death. One is taken, the other is saved. Is it just fortune? Is it just serendipity?

Often we cannot give an explanation for why one terrible thing happens to one person and not to the next. Is it because one person is upright and the other is evil? That was what Job's friends thought. Sometimes that explanation has some validity. But you don't have to live very long to discover that very bad things often happen to very good people. Is it the case that all of them are actually evil but only appear hypocritically to be good in the eyes of others? That is not very likely.

The harshest criticism God levels in the book of Job is not to Job himself, but to his presumptuous friends who think they have solved the problem of evil and suffering. They believed that if someone is suffering, then that person must be wicked. They thought this was true whether anyone could detect wickedness or not. Job's friends believed that suffering is proof that apparently good people are actually bad people. According to God, however, those guys flunked the theology test pretty badly.

By the way, there is a group of preachers and televangelists in our world today who believe the same thing Job's friends believed. If you are a

Christian and you are also poor or sick, then it is because you don't have the faith to get out of your poverty or illness. You are sinful, therefore, because of your lack of faith. Such teaching has done irreparable harm to the church of our Lord, and in the last few decades it has devastated the faith and hope of countless Christian people who were taught to believe what the preacher says. That is a bogus theology, and it is not found in the Bible or in historic orthodox Christian thought. But it was the type of thinking done by the friends of Job, a bunch God roundly rebuked. Sometimes there just is no easily acquired reason for explaining why suffering comes into the lives of God's people. Suffering does not always come with detailed explanations. But because it is not always self-explanatory, this does not mean we have to be completely silent in the face of it.

In the ninth chapter of the gospel of John, Jesus encounters a man born blind. As the Galilean is walking past the man, the disciples see an opportunity for some theological reflection. So, they ask Jesus "was this man born blind because of his parents' sin or because of his own sin?" Now, if you think about it, at least half of that question seems at least a little bit crazy. We might imagine a person could be born with a physical defect because of his parents' sin. In our own day there are many accounts of babies born to drug dependent or alcoholic parents and such babies may very well have birth defects that follow them all their lives. That half of the question makes a certain amount of sense. But how could someone be born blind as a result of his or her own sin?

The rabbis of Jesus' day believed that a baby could sin in the womb. There may be a mother reading this book who would say, "Yes, I believe that. My little rascal of a son gave me fits the last four months of my pregnancy, and he is still doing so today!" That may be true, but unless I am missing something, it is hard to imagine a sleeping baby in the womb actually capable of sinning.

It is probably the case that some Jewish people in first century Palestine thought that blessing was a sign of faithfulness and a curse was a sign of unfaithfulness. Therefore, if the man was born blind, it had to be due to someone's sin. That was the theology of Job's friends, but now in John chapter nine it has been adopted by Jesus' own disciples. But notice that Jesus does not attempt to deal with the theological question at all. Instead the Lord simply says, "This happened so that the work of God might be displayed in his life." Then he heals the man.

What is going on here? I think it is quite simple: We may not have an answer as to why the man is blind. There may not even be an answer. But the important thing is not to answer the question "why?" The important thing is to answer the question "what do we do now?" Whatever the correct theology of suffering might or might not be, the fact is we can act in a redemptive fashion in the middle of our suffering. Jesus then hammers that idea home when he says, "as long as it is day, we must do the work of him who sent me. Night is coming, when no one can work." Put in other words, let's get busy doing the work of God. Life is not over yet.

The unfortunate reality is that in this life we are promised trials. Easy answers to the problems associated with suffering are generally not correct answers. In C.S. Lewis's *The Great Divorce*, the visitor to the land of the Bright People is told that "what concerns you is the nature of the choice itself." In other words, how we respond is what is important.

In 1987 Debbie and I joined a unique, close-knit church. We felt affirmed there and the loving people of that congregation opened their arms to this somewhat different couple who were struggling to cope with an intractable illness. It was great for us, and we came to love both the pastor and people very dearly. Later, in the early 1990s, we became involved with a disability ministry that brought us deep joy and fulfillment. We led retreats for disabled people, and God was marvelous in giving us a ministry out of our ordeal. He always wants to do that in our lives if we will simply cooperate with the Plan. That ministry to the disabled was in itself part of a realized vision, a dream we had held for a long time.

In the midst of all of this, our dream of that new house especially designed for Debbie came true. While the design and much of the work were things I did with my own imagination and by my own hands, the fulfillment of this goal was only possible because of God's gifts of determination and perseverance built into me over the years of struggle. I think that is usually the way of it. The supernatural and the natural weave together in our lives so that all is from above, and yet it is accomplished through us here below, weak and fragile jars of clay that we are. It seems to me that often today God works in manners of intensity and timing more than in an outright spectacular supernatural anomaly. That is certainly how it happened in our experience.

As Debbie slowly got back to our version of "normal" after the problems related to the tube insertion, I slowly worked on the house, preparing it for her. I sought advice from others in determining the décor of the new house. You might say my talent was not in making things match, so Deb's mom helped with the interior decoration—such things as the curtains and adding a ladies' touch throughout. Of course the results that we described to her brought smiles to my dear wife.

It was the ideal house. I later gave her an anniversary gift of a large arch window. I installed it above her bed so that God's sunlight would pour in on her. That window was a living metaphor of what God was doing through Debbie, as he provided a window through which his light spilled all around her. We saw our entire home as a parable of the ultimate reality that our real home is in eternity. There the light always shines and is never dimmed by the darkness shrouding this age in which we live.

Everyone who knew Debbie could see the peace and contentment God brings to someone who seemingly has nothing really to live for. A friend named Kara wrote a poem expressing what people saw in Debbie. Here it is:

My Favorite Smile

She smiles when her husband speaks
it never fades throughout the weeks.
Although no sound from her lips is heard
her smile speaks a thousand words.
A radiant face with joy pours out
more so than with a jump or shout.
It's plain and clear for all to see
that in her life God's grace has set her free.
She rests within her Father's care
although she is confined within the chair.
The example she's been to me is sure

it's rest and peace and trust so pure.
She knows that God is in control
her body is sick but her spirit is whole
your faithfulness to God is true
in Debbie I thank God for you

My calling also became clear at that time. I already was confident my job was to be the husband to Debbie God wanted me to be. He was also calling me to a ministry that would take me farther in service than my wife's bedside. I was finally seeing the bigger picture.

Chapter 10

A Special Sister and Friend

⤳❦☙

Taking Up the Towel of Service

ISN'T IT AMAZING how the Holy Spirit responds to the desires of our hearts? At times we may know God wants us to do something but we can't express specifically what we think it is. In those moments the Holy Spirit begins to move us, getting us involved in surprising new adventures in loving his people. Opportunities to serve, support, and just be friends with others in painful circumstances began to come our way. We started a disability ministry in our church.

Our relationships with others who were suffering brought us deep joy and satisfaction as we realized the blessing of "comforting others with the comfort we received" (2 Corinthians 1:3–7). The beautifully simple truth of the principle that *it's in giving that we receive* was coming alive in our life experience as so much more than mere participation in "group therapy."

At weeklong disability ministry retreats we joined together and made special lifetime friends with many dear people. One such was Neal, who faced unspeakable challenges. Bedridden and severely contorted with cerebral palsy since birth, Neal lived faithfully into his eighties. I could always count on him to correct my New International Version Bible verses with his extensive mind-held database of the King James Version. Bob was always there, too. Bob was a big, strapping Italian man with a

119

rough Brooklyn accent. He had served in Vietnam. The Agent Orange herbicide defoliant that was sprayed on him by our own government caused Bob a lifetime of paralysis, as it did with other American heroes. He would often sacrificially make a trip over to serenade Debbie, literally crawling into our home and dragging his keyboard by the cord along the floor. Then there was the mother who mistakenly administered destructive medication to her now vegetative toddler. She tried to cope with the pain and guilt as her little son seemed perplexed and stared up into her eyes. I cannot forget, as well, the young deacon whose body was left in lifelong spastic contortion after being struck by lightning at a church picnic. The list goes on and on. Suffering comes in more varieties, shapes and sizes than you can imagine, that is unless you have had to stare it straight in the face and cope with it.

More doors began to open. One year I had the privilege of leading the concert of prayer and being part of a workshop panel discussion at a retreat for the disabled. The audience was encouraged to ask questions. The panel included Joni Eareckson Tada and her husband Ken Tada, Mark and Debbie Grawehr (imagine that!), and a mother with a disabled child.

I was then given the opportunity to be Director of Disability Ministries at Jacksonville Chapel, a large church in our community. Once a month we had Sunday afternoon dinners and Bible studies, and we would then go out and visit people who were disabled. We even sponsored an annual retreat. I was also serving in an AIDS ministry. I look back amazed at how God's grace made my nightmare a joy and how I began to learn how much there is to receive by simply giving! The promises I sensed God giving me when I first I became a Christian were coming to fruition.

A typical Sunday dinner ministry day for us would go something like this. After a refreshing "hot tub" bath, Debbie's nurse aide and I would get her ready to go out for the day. Hair curled, earrings on, ballerina shoes in place, we would then make a gentle transfer to Debbie's sheepskin-cushioned wheel chair. Her hands held on to silky hand rolls so that she had something to grip and again prevent her nails from digging into her palms as her spasms made her hands contract. Off we went, with me praying aloud as we drove (eyes open, of course!) to spend the afternoon with other friends who were trapped within bodies of precious but shattered clay. I'd glance into the back seat and hold Debbie's leg or foot to comfort her. Her wheelchair was strapped firmly to the floor of the van. She'd make her sounds, agreeing with my prayer for wisdom that God's love would flow through us to minister to hurting people.

Once we arrived I'd wheel my Beeba down the long sidewalk. As we approached the all-purpose building where our ministry event was housed, we would smell the mouth-watering, taste-bud-teasing aromas of some delicious cooking. We'd hear chattering in the kitchen and see people bustling around, finishing last minute touch-ups before everyone arrived. As they all begin to gather, we knew that for the next couple of hours there would be lots of joy, and some undeniable sadness.

We would likely hear that one of our friends was back in the hospital facing complications with his or her condition. We might discover that another person had been placed in a permanent care facility in another city, and might never be able to return to our fellowship events. It was also possible we might receive the news that a dear member of our group had been called home by the Lord since we last met. These were times of both laughter and tears, sometimes over the same piece of news.

Small busses and vans would begin to pull up in front of the building. Friends and family members of our disabled friends would help them out of their vehicles, and usher them inside for the event. Often they would stay and participate so that they became as much a part of our fellowship as their hurting loved one.

We would vary the themes of our meetings. Sometimes it might be Mexican, and both food and décor would mirror that. Another time the theme might be carnival, or learning about God's creation. The idea was to have a really good time and also to talk about some serious and important issues. We also made sure to share the gospel, since some of those who came to our meetings were spiritual seekers, not yet in the kingdom of God. We really welcomed those people and saw our ministry in part as helping them find reconciliation with God, a God whom some of them blamed for their terrible condition.

Debbie and I felt at home with these people. We would interact with friends who had no arms or legs, people twisted on their stretchers, others walking with canes or braces on their legs, each one seen by his or her Creator as someone special and someone loved. Some were overwhelmed with life and were simply trying to comprehend, to figure out where God fits into all of this. Others there were eager to share just how God had made himself real to them in the midst of their pain, suffering, and sorrow.

Someone who did not know better might have glanced into that room where we gathered and wondered who all of these strange, and often smelly, people were. I was reminded of what Scripture says in 1 Samuel 22:2. When David was driven out of Jerusalem by Saul, everyone in distress, everyone who was discontented or maladjusted in Israel, all went out to join David in the wilderness. And as we know from the rest of the story, this group became the core of a mighty army David would one day build, one with which he would sweep away the enemies of Israel after he became king. In a sense, that's what we experienced during our disability ministry. We had the kind of people who might not be considered *"GQ* Christians," not exactly fashion plates, but they loved the Lord and one another, and they became a mighty army in spiritual things.

When we were all together Walfredo would strum his guitar and quietly start a song that would soon spread. Before long we'd all be lifting our voices, some gratingly, some whose words were unrecognizable, some whispering, others, like my Beeba, sighing to the sounds, even though unable to articulate in words. For several, this singing was difficult, but they'd sing nonetheless. They focused on the goodness of our Creator God who forms each of us and knows us by name. Tears would often dampen cheeks at times as each of our hearts resounded praises to the glory of God. "Though he slay me, yet will I trust him" (Job 13:15) was one of the common attitudes shared by our friends.

Of course, others struggled to arrive at an honest understanding of their predicament because they were not yet convinced that God was a completely good God. We were so glad they came as well, and we prayed it would be there, perhaps that very day, that they would respond in faith to the gospel message and understand Jesus' suffering on their behalf.

Someone would pray and then I'd be asked to come up and share a word with the group. Debbie would be right next to me. Though I was the one reading the Scripture, and often we found ourselves turning to the story of Job, Debbie would "speak more loudly" even than I. Her facial expressions and her cooing sounds demonstrated to everyone there what she felt about the words I was speaking. Sometimes she'd sit quietly and peacefully. Then she might offer a mild grunt meaning "amen," or beam with one of her beautiful smiles and a "Debbie laugh." I recall times her ravaged body would spasm in pain and at the very moment I taught about God's view of suffering, she was experiencing it.

It was very important to have her beside me as I taught because Debbie became *Exhibit 1* of everything I tried to convey. Those who came to know us knew we were walking through the very fires I spoke about. Others who were there for the first time or who were skeptical about our faith could see this was not merely theory for us, and they could also see on my wife's face that she had truly learned how to face adversity by faith in Jesus Christ. She became a beacon of hope to others trapped in painful circumstances.

I used to think of myself at times as an "Aaron" and my wife as a modern "Moses." In the Old Testament book of Exodus, Aaron, who was the brother of Moses, would speak for his brother because Moses considered himself inarticulate. I was the one who brought the word in those services, but it was really Debbie who received the word from the Lord in her own pain. I shared what God was teaching both of us in the furnace of suffering. She brought mute testimony to the truth that suffering is not all there is to life. There is wholeness, completeness, and joy to be experienced in spite of the encroaching limitations that illness, pain, and the issues of life bring our way. Debbie's beauty in Christ pointed to the Man of Sorrows, the One who knows every pain. Because Jesus knew the greatest pain and suffering, he could therefore provide consolation to those ravaged by sickness.

After the teaching and singing, we'd all sit down to a wonderful meal. Time wasn't an issue in this group because we all understood that balancing plates on wheelchairs, eating with one's feet, and using feeding tubes all were part of the beauty of working together. Spills were the norm, and it was not unusual to be speaking with someone whose face was covered from side to side with food. One day Brooklyn Bob's leg spasmed, jolting the entire table forcefully upward and providing quite a memorable "manna from heaven" demonstration. Laughter was a gift we enjoyed.

Our joy increased as we identified with and invested our time in these other broken pilgrims, eagerly awaiting that city with foundations whose architect and builder is God (Hebrews 11:10). We would look toward that celestial city where there will no longer be any need for sun, moon, or stars, because everlasting light will be provided by God himself. We would praise God both with words and without, in whatever way we were able to do so, knowing that when we are in the presence of God, we will no longer be earthen vessels cracked and stained with sin and suffering, but instead we will be glorified vessels, showing the greatness of God's grace to the watching world and the principalities and powers of the universe. We will finally be without spot or wrinkle, a pure bride for the heavenly Bridegroom.

Alongside these fellow children of God, these disabled ones whose vessels showed every sign of cracking and pressure, we knew that one day we would all return to the dust of the earth, for from dust we were made. Yet, together we felt energized by God's continuous washing and renewal day by day. We fixed our gaze together on the glorious Master Potter and together we built one another up and encouraged one another in our pilgrimage of faith. That encouragement was extremely important to all of us, since, as I have mentioned before, suffering people often find themselves isolated or at best spending time with only a small circle of people who are part of their lives. This fellowship enabled all of us to recognize we were part of a larger community.

When the Bible speaks of church, it generally refers to a local community of believers gathered for the purpose of teaching, ministry to one another and encouragement. God wants to fill our lives in a vertical fashion—with himself and through his Spirit (Ephesians 5:18)—but there is a horizontal aspect to that filling. In the ancient church there were "anchorites," hermit monks who moved to some remote location and lived in solitude, believing God called them to a lonely life of prayer and spiritual warfare. One of these was Anthony, a fourth century Egyptian who at the age of twenty gave away all his possessions and went to live in the Egyptian desert. For many years he stayed in an abandoned fortress, and for many of those years he was completely alone, wrestling with the devil, sometimes standing in the form of a cross for hours on end. Over time, he acquired legendary status, and other young men began to come out to join him in the wilderness. This was not what Anthony had in mind, so he encouraged them to find their own place of solitude.

Anthony is considered by many to be a kind of hero of the Christian faith. There is no doubt that he was a man deeply dedicated to God. But that kind of dedication is not germane to the average Christian, nor ought it to be. God has made us as social beings, and communal nature is the norm. Not only is it the norm, it is the mechanism by which we are enabled to live in community with other believers. We need that outward community every bit as much as we need to know God in the inner recesses of our own hearts. Knowing God, then, is more than just meditation, prayer, and Bible reading; it is also knowing Christ in other people. That requires community.

There is also something to be said for Christian community with people sharing some unique quality. There are Christian motorcycle fellowships, Christian cowboy fellowships, and even Christian hot air ballooning fellowships. I am sure those groups are a lot of fun for people who enjoy those pursuits. People who have disabilities and who join a ministry like ours or like Joni and Friends do so for the enjoyment it brings, but also for more serious reasons. It is just helpful to be around others struggling with similar problems, and who have found ways to be victorious in their lives through those problems. Those people were very precious to Debbie and me in those days, and they still are. Ecclesiastes 4:12 says that a three-stranded cord is not easily broken. Strength comes to those banding and bonding together around the work of the Spirit of God shared mutually in their hearts.

A Friend in Need, a Friend in Deeds

We saw God's hand at work when some of Debbie's private nurses came to some of those gatherings at Jacksonville Chapel. This allowed me the chance to minister and connect with them as something more than simply their employer. It was also about this time I was asked to lead a group of men in a discussion and study about how to love their disabled wives more deeply. This happened at a retreat for disabled families in Pennsylvania.

God's hand continued to work, because also about this time a young woman named Becky, who grew up on the mission field in Papua New Guinea, had just arrived at our church. Ministering to missionary kids was an emphasis in our church. We wanted to give them a place to adapt and assimilate to American culture. We met Becky previously at another gathering where she was very drawn to Debbie and really seemed to connect well. She often spoke with her after church, whereas most other people found it difficult to relate to my wife. Becky first came to our church from an international missions organization called New Tribes Mission. I remember the first time I noticed this cute red-headed girl who really looked like she had the joy of the Lord in her heart. After she graduated from New Tribes Bible Institute in Michigan, Becky came to work with the youth in our church.

One of her first nights in town she came to the care group meeting in our home. She clearly admired us as a couple and had a deep appreciation for how we had endured our struggles. We found as time went on that Becky was seeking answers to questions that internally nagged her. Being deeply wounded at a young age, Becky's view of God and God's love for her was challenging the very core of her faith.

As a missionary child, Becky had a very traumatic experience as she was being raised in the primitive Aziana tribe. At four years old she was severely abused by one of the indigenous people to whom her family was ministering, a man who threatened to kill her if she told anyone what had happened. She lived with that on her conscience and in her memory all the way through high school and beyond. That affected her view of men, and even made it difficult for her to think of a prospective husband. Not until she was a teenager did she finally confide in someone as to what had happened; she lived all those years in silent mortification and guilt over this traumatic event.

Becky was to become an extremely important part of our lives over the next several years. Here is her recollection of our first meeting:

> Knock, knock, knock. I sprang up from my sleeping bag, exhausted from the twelve-hour drive through the night. I'd had only a few

hours of sleep, and I was upset. A glance in the mirror revealed a puffy face and swollen eyes, swollen from lack of sleep . . . and from crying. The first question that came to mind was, "Where am I?" My clouded mind had to take a quick inventory.

"Hello, who is it?"

"It's me. Tim. Hurry, Becky, I want you to meet a very special couple, Mark and Debbie Grawehr. They will be here in a little while in the backyard for Kara's sister's baby dedication. You've got to meet them . . . especially Debbie."

"Okay," I responded, as my thoughts jerked me back to the heartache that continued to gnaw at me.

Why had I come here? That perplexing question recurred through the next moments as I quickly dressed and prepared myself to go out and meet them. I had followed Tim to this place. Tim was my high school boyfriend, someone I just loved to be around, someone who understood, someone I hoped maybe to marry. But something had gone terribly wrong. Tim was now dating Kara, and they seemed to be very serious in their relationship. I had followed them to this place out of a sense of desperation. What else could I do?

The truth was that my heart was breaking inside me. The pain of it flooded my mind. "I don't understand," I lamented to the silence that surrounded me. I hurt deep inside. "Where do you find answers and healing especially when you can't understand why you are going through the hurt in the first place?" The emptiness in my heart prodded me with a lurking reminder. "Help! I know there is a God who *can* come to my rescue. But will he? And how? "

When I was four years old I acknowledged Christ as my Savior. I was always grateful for that, and I knew it was the most important single event in my life. But I really wanted to *know him*. And similar to the woman who had internal bleeding (Mark 5:21-34) as she came up behind Jesus in the crowd, I wanted to know his healing touch. I needed to know him in the secret places where I hurt.

People in the Bible talked about really knowing God. I knew of course that most of them had not known God in the way that we know other people. That is, they did not sit down and have a conversation with him the way you have a conversation with your brother or your boss. Some of them actually did know God like this, but even in the Bible that was an exception. I was not naive about that, and I was not looking for some kind of mystical and otherworldly experience to stimulate my emotions.

Knowing God is not like going to a coffee shop with someone and I did not merely want emotional experiences that had no substance. But what I did want was to know God and not just know about him. I had seen the Lord work in people's lives, including my own, or at least I believed I had. But now I faced my own grown-up spiritual dilemma. The question I was facing was "Is God really here?" In Hebrews 11 it says that anyone who comes to God must believe that he exists. . . I had to ask myself, "Does God really exist? . . . And if he does exist, is he really good?" Questions loomed in my head as my mind flashed back to times when, as a little girl, I would be slumped in a corner engaged in a battle of having to cope with my secret trauma. So shaken and afraid, I told no one. Even then, I was sometimes tempted to think, "God really doesn't love you, not really, or he wouldn't have allowed the pain." I would then go on to reflect, "I've heard that God loves me. I so hope he loves me. My head knows it but my heart longs to know it. But then I'd wonder why he did not make that love more clear to me in the middle of my own inner anguish, in the here and now. I knew he died and rose for me, but there was a disconnect I wish wasn't there.

"I know!" I spoke out loud. "I know what I've been taught. I know what I've seen, but I have to find him personally in the midst of pain somehow." Here was my last thin piece of thread, my last glimmer of hope. No one had ever known this raging battle within that I had fought for years. I walked the best I knew as a Christian, but I knew I couldn't go back to the mission field this way. "Help me, Lord," I whispered, saying goodbyes just the day before. I had completed two years of Bible school and now, moving to New Jersey, I was opening a new chapter in my life. New people, a new location—it was all new to me again. And yet, because of my aching heart I felt numb. A new chance to work with children as I searched for him would keep my focus on their needs not mine.

As I threw myself together that Sunday afternoon, I peered through the big glass window of lush greenery contrasting with a white fence bridge. Huddled in groups, talking freely, was a collection of smiling people. What a beautiful backyard, I thought, and what apparently happy people, as my mind wandered over the scene that stood before me. This couple—Mark and Debbie—why did Tim even care for me to meet them, anyway? Where is this Debbie and what does she look like and what will it be like here? Will this be a place that will be home where I will be settled or yet another transition home? What is home anyway?

I went down what seemed to be a maze of stairs and joined Tim and Kara, as I walked to the backyard in tired anticipation. Meeting new people was always out of my comfort zone. You are supposed to be friendly and warm, yet you never know if you will actually "connect." Would there be a connection this time, or would it simply be another awkward introduction sending me looking for a convenient escape? Tim led me over through the crowd to meet Mark and Debbie.

Approaching them, it was all I could do not to stare, stunned. I was completely taken aback, like a deer caught in the stark glare of an automobile's headlights. I stood, my eyes glued to Debbie. There she was, captivating, yet unnatural, beauty beaming through her bent drooling smile. Her clear blue eyes glistened as one drifted to the right and reverted back, seemingly trying to focus. Her hands gripped the wash cloths rolled within her palms, her hands stiffening as her body spasmed involuntarily and uncontrollably. She sat in her wheelchair with pillows, and with one leg rested unevenly on the foot pedal. One thin leg was lower than the other and at the end of each leg appeared to be white ballerina shoes, obviously chosen for their softness and for the fact that they were easy to put on and take off. The shoes sat comfortably on her feet, but her feet did not appear to be comfortable on the foot rests, as they were uneven and contorted. Her emaciated body tilted to the side, resulting from the effects of something I already knew about—curvature of the spine, or scoliosis.

Drooling as she smiled, Debbie almost seemed to try to make contact with me. Mark tenderly wiped her face with a cloth. "Mark and Debbie, this is Becky Dodd. She's a missionary friend I grew up with in Papua New Guinea," Tim said.

I struggled to refocus and smiled, trying not to show the questions flooding my mind. Mark greeted me with a warm smile as he played with Debbie's ear lobe, all the while rubbing her arm. "Hi, Becky, it is nice to meet you," Mark offered. Debbie then groaned with an apparent sense of pleasure.

This was my first encounter with a man and a woman who would be instrumental in changing my life, as well as the lives of many people around me. Little did I suspect that fateful day would be filled with its own anxieties and tortures, nor that I was entering a relationship that would see those frustrations come to an end. I didn't know this yet but I would ultimately become nurse to this exceptional woman, and yet, in a sense, it would be the very presence within her that would nurse me back to spiritual and emotional health. Luke 4:23, although in a different context, would come to be true in my life—"Physician, heal thyself." Healing would certainly come to me, but not in the way I could have imagined.

As she got to know Debbie, Becky appreciated her even more and wanted to spend time with her. People who took the time to learn to communicate with Debbie were often attracted to her, since she had a wonderful spirit of humility and love. Becky had a similar spirit about her, and it may well be that each woman was formed and molded by their own crises. Debbie was molded by an illness that was the most apparent thing anyone would have noticed about her. This formed her into a spiritual woman of prayer, love, and humility. Becky also was formed and molded by her own crisis, one that was less obvious to the casual observer, but one which ultimately moved her from insecurity to becoming a woman of love and sensitivity, and one with a passion for service. In Debbie she had an immediate opportunity for Christian service—giving emotional, physical, and spiritual care to a physically helpless woman. Yet, Becky would discover something I had already learned. She would discover that a relationship with Debbie was decidedly a two-way street, and that Debbie brought even more to the friendship than anyone might expect, physically handicapped though she was.

Before long Becky became Debbie's best friend. I have no way to express to you just how important this was to me. I had prayed for such a dear friend for my wife for years. Debbie had always had her mother and me in her life, and we were always there for her. But in a way we were sort of expected to be there for her. What she had never had was someone, especially a devoted sister in Christ, who had no family ties to her who still wanted to be close in this special way.

Since the illness began, Debbie never had anything quite like this friend. People were *friendly*, but no one was a real true *friend*. Those are very different things. One does not need a lot of friends, but one does need true friends. As Samuel Johnson once said, "true happiness consists not in the multitude of friends, but in their worth and choice." Now Debbie had someone who wanted to be with her, not out of a sense of guilt, or obligation, or neediness, but out of true friendship. This was one of the best things that had happened to Debbie since the illness began.

Becky loved Debbie because Debbie was a person worthy of love. Becky found that as she grew closer to her, the more she was drawn to both Debbie and God. Debbie leveraged the privilege of her seemingly purposeless existence in moment by moment surrendered communion with the Holy Spirit of God. Since she had been with God somehow when you were with her you also felt closer to God himself. As we die to self and put on our righteousness in Christ, we become more like him. The philosopher Socrates once said that we love that which we perceive to be good. Goodness calls forth our love. I think that he was very perceptive.

As Becky's friendship with Debbie grew she became part of our disability ministry team. We asked if she'd consider coming with us to the retreat to assist with Debbie's care needs. At that retreat, Becky had the opportunity to meet Joni, whose book she had read some years before.

When I was needed to be more involved in ministering specifically to someone in the disability ministry, Becky was there to help with Debbie. This enabled me to be a blessing to others also in need of ministry and care. Becky would confide in Debbie, telling her things she had never told anyone. She saw Debbie as a trusted friend. Becky came to know that even if Debbie could talk, she would never have broken any confidence with respect to anything Becky had shared with her. A major prayer of my heart had been that we could find a genuine friend, a sister in the Lord to Debbie. Becky was God's clear answer to my prayers.

A Caring Friend, a Loving Nurse

After being in the States a while, Becky decided to become a nurse. She went to school to obtain the necessary training, knowing of the compelling need in missions overseas. Her friendship with us evolved while she was in the process of nurse's training. After she graduated I asked her if she would be willing to care for Debbie on a regular basis. Another answer to prayer! She turned out to be exactly what we had needed all of those years. The "burden" of caring for my wife became more and more bearable all the time.

As difficult as it is to walk the MS path we walked for the prior years, what had always made it more difficult was that I often simply did not know what was going on at my house while I was at work. I would be laboring over some figures or over the challenge of some new construction we were engaged in, and I would suddenly have a flash go through my mind. Is everything OK with Debbie? Is there a crisis I do not know about? Is her nurse treating her with respect or is she making my wife's day miserable? At times I just did not know the answers to those questions.

With Becky taking care of Debbie, all of that changed. When I would come home from work I would often find Debbie and Becky together, with Becky singing or praying. The atmosphere in the home was different from what it had been, deeper and more meaningful. Becky's heart was to help Debbie be all she could be as my wife. She always had Debbie looking beautiful when I would come home. She would often fix her hair, put on her makeup and dress her in her nicest clothes. Becky would then step into the background, leaving Debbie to greet me, beaming from ear to ear when I walked in the door.

Most of her nurses fulfilled the minimal requirements of caring for my wife, but most often they did little more than that. In many ways, Becky allowed Debbie the opportunity to feel feminine and pretty again and to bring joy to her husband. Becky had a servant's heart in helping Debbie fulfill these desires. In that way she gave herself selflessly to enhance our lives together. She was more than a nurse—she was a friend in deeds, and a friend indeed.

God has consistently exceeded my expectations in so many ways. I must admit, however, many of my prayers have been, to be frank, more than a little self-serving. But God has begun a good work in me, as the apostle Paul put it (Philippians 1:6), and in spite of my very evident humanness, God has answered my prayers in ways that go far beyond what I might have expected. He gave me the grace to be able to minister to other disabled people. He granted me remarkable success in my business. He also gave me a wonderful role model in my earthly father, who, unlike some of his distant ancestors, came from poverty to make something of himself. My father in turn set a great example of how to manage one's life and how important it is to work hard, and to invest wisely.

I see many of those principles taught in God's word. My friend Oleh quoted Joel 2:25 to me, which says, "I will repay you for the years the locusts have eaten." In Joel's time, before the fields could be harvested God sent a plague of locusts to consume the crops the Israelites were raising. God was judging the people for their sin and idolatry. This was devastating to the Israelites, who depended on the harvest for their very livelihood. But God later restored the prosperity lost in those years.

The difference between me and the prophet Joel is that we have lived our locust-eaten years after we turned to God, not before. We live in a fallen world. We have to expect that we will face the refining fire in one way or another at some point in our lives. For Debbie and me it came early in life, while for others those challenges wait for the later years. And I may certainly face that refinement in the future as well. God used that, and then exceeded my expectations of how he would guide us into serving others in ministry.

God exceeded my expectations of a nurse. I never dreamed when we met Becky and then hired her to help that I'd be able to hire my wife's new best friend. I had not even thought or imagined how good this could be. She rounded out our lives together and provided a sort of last piece of the puzzle that made our picture complete. She was from the outside, from a distant land, but she came to us and contributed hugely to making our lives together more meaningful than they had been before. Before was good between Debbie and me, but now it was even better.

Interestingly, as much as she was a blessing to us, we were also a blessing to Becky. We met a need in her life, and she would tell you her friendship with Debbie was life-changing. In fact, Debbie became the best friend Becky ever had. I guess that is to be expected. Friendships simply do not work if they go only one direction. Reciprocity is one of the things that makes friendships happen. Becky would tell you Debbie made a bigger difference in her life than anyone she had ever met, aside from her parents and the Lord himself.

This may be hard for people to understand, since it is so easy to overlook the fact that someone who is a complete invalid might also, if he or she has some way to communicate at all, be able to convey a heart and mind that is deep with passion, with devotion, and with love. Becky was discovering what I had already long known. Buried within the vessel's fragile outer coating was an increasingly godly woman who was participating more each day in the divine nature. The book of 2 Peter expresses this temporariness this way—it calls the physical body a "tent" (1:13), an impermanent structure that will be put aside.

Debbie's mind and her spirit were deeper and more profoundly real than those of almost anyone else I have ever met. But that mind and spirit were locked inside a body almost totally incapable of communicating with the world outside her frail frame. To those who were able to tap into that that communication, however, it was something special.

Hope for a Child?

Some time after Becky came to work with Debbie, around Mother's Day in 1994, they were both listening to Joni's radio show and heard of a medical institution in Philadelphia claiming huge success assisting disabled women with having children. When they heard this news, Debbie responded like never before. She replied with long groans, her eyes were pinned wide open, and through our communication flow chart she let Becky know that this was definitely something she wanted to pursue.

Like most women, Debbie had deeply desired to be a mother. She knew she would probably die young. But if only she could have a child, at least she could leave knowing that she had left her legacy to the world. But that did not appear to be a possibility, at least in this way. Furthermore, unlike most other childless women, Debbie had little to do most days except to sit and think about the implications of her illness and to sulk over the reality of it, though she did little of that. Still, I knew she wanted almost more than anything else to be a mom. Debbie of course could not tell me this directly, but ultimately she made it clear to Becky that she needed *her* to tell me about this. So one evening as I returned home, Becky mustered the courage to be Debbie's mouthpiece and lay it on me. She reluctantly approached me with Debbie's urgent hope, and as she did, Debbie grinned widely and began to moan pleadingly with excitement.

My heart sank. Then it soared. Maybe I could be a dad! But then reality hit again. I was very reluctant, since Debbie was so severely afflicted. And how could I ever deal with an infant, a child, a teenager and so on?! I would need to raise this child alone. I was not sure I was up to such a task. But I could not ignore her desire. I knew this barrenness had hurt her for many years. She had so much wanted a child! So, in spite of my fears, I pursued the possibility as fully as I could.

I spoke to the chief obstetrician at the medical center and he advised me of the many risks, but also said he thought it was at least possible. I was stunned. Here was my wife, thirty-seven years old, paralyzed from the neck down, legally blind, unable to speak, and yet still with the chance to have a child? When I counseled with some others, they told me they suspected that maybe the obstacles could be overcome. By this time, as I normally did with big decisions, I called upon my fellow deacons and the elders at our church and sought their counsel. They were cautious and reluctant to give strong encouragement to us to attempt the process, and yet they were at the same time supportive.

I was hopeful though skeptical. In fact, I was excited. At the same time I could not help but think to myself, "This is crazy!" The idea that Debbie and I could have a child in the deteriorated condition of her body after all these years of the illness! It was something to think about. But like the men at my church, I was cautious. More than that, I did not want her to be disappointed yet again. I sent medical records and even a videotape of her condition. We had an MRI done that showed severe damage to Debbie's brain and spinal column. Through the entire process we held out our hopes, though deep in my heart I feared the final word would be "no."

Shortly thereafter, a medical team gave the opinion that she would probably not survive and also that the child might not endure, either. In fact, they were surprised Debbie was even alive, that she had lived all these years and was still able to function and communicate. How could I tell Debbie this devastating news?

Here was my beloved bride who had had only a short time with me in any kind of normal married life, permanently robbed of the ability to do for me most of the kinds of things she had always wanted to do. This terrible disease had stolen from her the ability to enjoy and appreciate life and the good things that came our way. With the exception of the first months of our life together, we had never been able to enjoy watching a mountain sunset. She could not whisper into my ear all of the romantic things that were in her heart as she thought about the love she had for her husband. She loved to sing. She might have once sung to me one of her favorites, "I Love You Just the Way You Are" by Billy Joel. Now however, she longed to sing the great hymns of the faith that she had learned mostly since she had lost the ability to speak. But she could only listen and sing them in her heart, and she did, with greater fervor and more passion than almost anyone enjoys in public worship. All of these things had been denied her. Now, after getting her hopes up, she would be disappointed again.

We believed, of course, that the Master Potter had been at work in all of that, and that none of it was a surprise to him, nor beyond his ability to transform. Yet even that conviction did not lessen our longing to have something together in our marriage that would belong to us. Even knowing that God has a vast eternal plan did not dampen our desire to share every scrap of hope and joy we could possibly muster. To have a child! That would have meant everything to my beloved. The glimmer of hope we had been given—that little crack of the door open to a room filled with wonders had created joyful expectations that very few people can possibly understand. And now, I was going to have to slam that door shut.

So many doors had been slammed shut in front of her over the years, and I had often had to be the one to break the news that another possibility had been dashed; another hopeful dream had to be abandoned. I cannot even convey the dread I had of facing that moment. If you have ever hated to make a certain phone call, to knock on a specific door, to walk into a meeting at work or some other place, knowing that this was the one conversation you did not want to have, then perhaps you can have some sense of how I felt.

I gently gave her the news that the medical team had given to me. She communicated as passionately as she could that she really wanted to try anyway. She soon realized then I could not go there. Her sobs of disappointment nearly broke my heart. Quickly however, the tears subsided and a smile emerged. I saw on her face that though this news was so very hard, she now was content. Her attitude spoke deeply to my own soul of much more God wanted to teach me through her life!

A Scripture came to me at that moment: "Godliness with contentment is great gain" (1 Timothy 6:6). Debbie was content with the Lord's will. He was the Master and he was molding her future. We can dream our dreams, but if it becomes clear they are not part of the Potter's plan for our lives, then we can abandon them and still be content. That is the case because we know he has good things in store for those who love him, for those who are called according to his purpose (Romans 8:28). It reminded me that the real miracles in life often are not physical ones, but the miracles worked in the heart by the Holy Spirit.

From a theological point of view, maybe we ought not to call them "miracles" in any technical sense. But what I mean is that it takes a dramatic work of the Holy Spirit in our lives to save us, to transform us, to make us happy with what the Lord brings into our lives along the way. It is not as dramatic as splitting the Red Sea and not as significant as the resurrection of Jesus from the dead. But it is still a work of God, and it always leaves the divine fingerprint on us. So, even as God left his fingerprint on a patch of water in the Middle East and another one on a stone cold tomb in a garden in Jerusalem, he leaves fingerprints on our hearts every time he does a transforming work.

God has the power to change the physical world and can do so in an instant if it pleases him. Changing a heart is an even greater thing, and shows that God truly can and does still work those miracles every day. He did such a thing in the life of my wife that dark day when I had to inform her that another hope was now lost. He had been doing it ever since we first met him, and he wasn't about to be finished yet. We were in his loving hands. We would feel them molding us and shaping us into his image in weeks and months to come.

Chapter 11

Sojourners in God's Land

⌐⫯⊙

Summer 1995

EVERY YEAR FOR vacation we'd rent a motor home and get away—just the two of us. We'd find a spot and I'd bundle Debbie up and set her in a chair next to the campfire. We usually did not go far since I was always concerned we might have an emergency and I wanted to be close to the doctors who knew her condition better than anyone else. But one of our dreams had been to make a journey out west, to see the national parks and other sights we'd seen in pictures and had heard so much about. So in September of 1995, we decided to do something special and take a big trip to the western United States.

I restored an old dilapidated and disgustingly orange motor home with a friend. It had a raised bed by a large side window that I could strap her into so she could sense as much of the scenery as she could. The bed was locked into place right behind the drivers' seat, so I could drive the motor home with my left hand and reach behind me to hold my Beeba's foot with the other. Those were truly remarkable days for us, and among my fondest memories.

The morning we left it was raining. Accompanying us in this "big adventure" was Debbie's mother Florence, and her nurse and friend Becky. This was her "inner circle." As we drove along, Deb's mom made sandwiches for us and we explained to Debbie what we were seeing. It was a very special time for all of us. We marveled at the magnificent grandeur of the Rockies, at the clean brilliance of Yellowstone River, at the power and presence of Old Faithful. That brought pleasure to my wife. She was excited to hear of the things she had always heard about, as anyone is who makes such a trip out West, but I'm sure she was also a little bit frustrated that she had such limited ability to enjoy and appreciate what she was experiencing. One would never have detected that frustration, though, since she was so obviously joyful at the progress of our adventure.

I remember her wistful expression. I imagine that like others with disabilities confronted with such an opportunity to see such magnificence; she wanted to leap out of her confining body and experience wonderful things. She wanted to feel what it would be like to take off her shoes and wade in the crystal clear streams that are so common in the Rocky Mountains—to savor the cold, clean water rushing through her toes and up past her ankles. She longed to get out of her chair and hike up a trail to the top of a peak, to stand there with the perspiration that comes from such a climb beading on her forehead, and then look out over the lovely valley below. She wished, I am sure, that she could wander out into those green meadows dotted with wildflowers, to pick a few of those blossoms and put them in her hair to wear for the rest of the day. I did bring some of those beautiful flowers back to her after picking some while running. I'd describe them to her and she would beam back at me with a big smile.

More than anything, I am confident she would have wanted to share the moments with me. She would certainly have loved the idea of looking into my eyes through the smoke of a late night camp fire, after having spent time gathering wood to build it. I am sure Debbie would have enjoyed putting her arm around me as we wormed our way around each other in the limited confines of the motor home, with a little romantic smile and a peck on the cheek.

Of course, she was able to do none of these things. So, our journey was joyous and sad, pleasant and yet frustrating all at the same time. It is often the case that the most difficult things in life still have some tinge of grace, while even the most joyous of experiences never completely escape the hint of a shadow of fear. Our time on that trip, though, was mostly happy and joyous.

On the trip Becky would read to us all as we cruised down the road breathing in the fresh mountain air, and then we'd sing. Debbie loved to listen to us sing. We cruised along the beautiful mountain highways singing songs like "Wind beneath My Wings." Debbie would beam with that wonderful and engaging smile that all of her friends and family had come to know so well. Have you ever known someone with such a smile that could transform any moment, melt any heart, and soften any sadness? Victor Borge said that a smile is the shortest distance between two people. Debbie could brighten up any room with that smile, and she brightened our trip every day. Her smile is still the thing that many people remember when I see them after a long absence.

There was a growing bond between Debbie and Becky, but also between Becky and me. We recognized, of course, that there was a line that could not be crossed. And neither of us wanted to cross that line. Ours was a friendship, a friendship centered primarily around one person—my wife and Becky's friend. She became like a younger sister to me. When we came to the various national parks we always went on different trails. This was not just for the sake of appearance, either. The cast of characters on our trip included Debbie's mother Florence, and of course she would have been hurt had she thought that anything more than a friendship was there between Becky and me.

We took different trails not just for Florence's sake, however, but because we knew that our relationship was one that centered on Debbie. That was who we were; that was what we wanted. Even more than that, we wanted to honor the Lord. Debbie knew this, of course. But she also knew that there had been many opportunities to succumb to temptation over the previous fifteen years because I had shared these temptations with her. I asked her from time to time to pray that God would keep me pure. Her prayers, as usual, were effective.

The people in that motor home were the ones closest to Debbie in the world. It was a foretaste of heaven for her because she had the opportunity to have uninterrupted fellowship with her most precious family and friend. That is part of what will make heaven, or the new heavens and new earth, to be quite biblical, the great thing it will be. We have all experienced the pain of loss—of grandparents, parents, siblings, friends, spouses, and others. Those losses will one day be forever behind us if those loved ones who went before us into eternity accepted in this life the forgiveness and eternal life that Jesus offers. We will also have fellowship with people who are completely and finally freed from sin, from inconsistencies, from frailty, and from all weaknesses. In this life we all still have "issues." That will eventually be no longer the case.

We did have several upsetting breakdowns on the trip. Just as dusk was approaching one evening, the motor home sputtered to a complete stop. There we sat, in the barren plain of Wyoming, in a big rig that was immobile. It would be hours before we could get any help. Eventually we found a tow truck and were hauled in to the closest mechanics shop. During the towing, I heard frequent squealing noises coming from the tow truck. After our arrival I got out of the motor home and asked the driver of the tow truck what the noise was. He replied that since the motor home was so heavy his front wheels would often become airborne and then hit the ground skidding to slow down!

Joni's book on heaven came out just before we made our trip. Becky and Florence read the book to Debbie during times when I would be dealing with some kind of mechanical issue. I believe that book was partly instrumental in helping Deb's mom come to a wonderful decision. She made her profession of faith in Christ. For years she had observed the faith of her daughter. She knew Debbie had been remarkably transformed in spite of, or even as a result of, her illness. She had watched that for years, but it was on this trip she decided to taste and see for herself the victorious life in spite of a mountain of difficulties that her daughter had.

When we pulled back into home Debbie's dad was waiting to meet us with open arms and hugs. He came into the motor home, and Debbie just groaned out to him, indicating what a wonderful time we had all experienced together during those two weeks. He smiled, knowing that every good time was a blessing for one who had suffered so much.

The trip was a hint of what heaven will be like for all of us. Of course, what we had no way of knowing was that for Debbie it was truly a foretaste of heaven, since her time with us was more limited than we knew. All that would become clear in the next couple of months.

Debbie's Missionary Journey

In 1995 we also attended Debbie's twentieth high school reunion. In previous years she had no desire to go to the reunions because she did not want people to see her in the condition her MS presented. But by now God freed her of her early self-consciousness. That was one of the more remarkable aspects of Debbie's spiritual growth and transformation. I will say it again, as wonderful as the miracles of the Bible are, and they truly are signs of God's power, another amazing indicator of God's powerful working in our lives is the transformation that comes about as the Lord who is Spirit conforms us more and more into Christ's image (2 Corinthians 3:18).

Though she was legally blind and had not seen herself in years, Debbie was under no illusion about the extent to which MS had ravaged her body. She wanted to go to that reunion so that together we could share what Christ had done in our lives over the past decade and a half. Much had transpired since her high school twirling days. Our values had changed and this was a missionary moment for her. It was an act of self-denial for the sake of the cross. She was able to respond to a higher calling of bearing witness to the grace and mercy of a God who had saved her, and who was always with her in spite of her condition.

Have you ever entered a room where a group of people were engaged in a lively conversation and it stops as soon as you walk in? That's the way it was at the reunion, multiplied by the number of people there. The experience was awkward, unusual, weird, and yet, profound. Debbie, the pretty high school twirler, had been popular but her classmates also knew she was not one to draw attention to herself. Yet there she was, and in a condition that this time could not help but attract very different kinds of stares and comments.

As the hours passed not just a few remarked about the deep inner beauty and contentment they saw in her. I think Debbie was a living example of 2 Corinthians 4:16b: "Though outwardly we are wasting away, yet inwardly we are being renewed day by day." I also think once again of that verse that captures Debbie's life more perhaps than any other: "We have this treasure in jars of clay to show that this all surpassing power is from God and not from us" (2 Corinthians 4:7). This glory never fades. All told, this reunion celebration was quite an evening. What a courageous thing to do.

In October of 1995 those of us close to Debbie began to realize her health was declining more significantly. Respiratory problems were assailing her. We had been percussing the back of her lungs for quite some time, but this was becoming ineffective in dealing with the problem. We knew that most people who have MS do not die of the disease, but rather they often can die of respiratory infections. This made us increasingly concerned about her health.

Becky and I took comfort in our friendship during this difficult time, but we were deeply purposed to not yield to any kind of temptation—mental, emotional, or physical. I was committed to my wife and my love for her transcended love for any other mortal being. Of course, my thoughts and actions were not then and are not now impeccable. I suppose no man's are. Once again Debbie was always the first to know from me that temptation was real, and she had been my first accountability partner.

Becky and I both knew that we needed help and encouragement in accountability. The problem was that we now knew we could not find that accountability any longer in our own church. We discovered about this time that our pastor failed morally. This was my pastor, the very man I looked up to as a spiritual guide and the one I looked to for accountability in my own struggles with temptation! And it is important for me to say that he made a very large and important impact on my life for the good. I suppose one of the lessons here is that even those whose lives are marked by spiritual failure are not incapable of helping people. I loved him then and still do today. But this was a huge disappointment to me and a real discouragement to our church. How could he have allowed such a thing to become part of his life? I felt I could no longer go to him for help. So, we sought out the assistance of another local pastor and a very close friend, among others. God provided the grace for us to continue to work together in assisting my beloved Debbie.

Becky and I were convinced we had to take the high road in regard to our relationship as friends. This was all the more true now. We loved my wife and we loved the Lord. We knew we could not let anything else stand in the way of those commitments. Becky spoke with her parents over the phone and told them what we were concerned about. We were both committed to give our hearts and lives to caring for my wife. But we were also committed not to give any place to the Devil. Wisely, her dad said it was time to come home. She did just what he told her to do. So, as the year 1995 waned to a close, I was again nursing my wife, often alone, through increasingly difficult days.

Debbie's condition was now rapidly deteriorating. She was choking more often, and we were having a more difficult time stopping the choking. Her lungs were always filled with congestion. Oxygen was always available by her bedside. Breathing was becoming progressively difficult. We had been battling this illness for over sixteen years. Now we began to face the fact that this delicate jar of clay was ready to shatter.

Chapter 12

Awaiting the Master Potter's Call

"You Have to Let Me Go"

IT WAS DECEMBER. Winter was just coming on and it was to be a winter of the heart as well as one of the seasons. Debbie and I had never before been as close as we were in those fading days of the year 1995. Our recent trip to the West was still part of our everyday communication. Christmas was approaching—always a time of joy and appreciation for the blessings we'd known together over the years. But something else was also going on, something not quite so pleasant.

Debbie had a clear sense that her health was declining and declining rapidly. She could feel it in her body. Though she had not been well in nearly seventeen years, she sensed that her body was falling into a tailspin that was different and irreversible. Meanwhile, I was continuing the fight to help her struggle on. That was becoming more and more difficult as each week marched by. On top of all this I was still dealing with the after effects of a crisis my business partner created that nearly tore our company apart.

I had heard of the movie *Shadowlands*, the story of the relationship of C. S. Lewis with his wife, Joy Davidman. Debbie and I watched the film together, just the two of us. We got to the scene where Joy, Lewis's wife, who had cancer, was battling for her life with the dread disease. Her husband was at her side, coaching her on, and encouraging her to continue the struggle. He was urging her to fight and to make her life last as long as she could by force of will alone, if possible. At that point in the film she looked at him and said simply, "You have to let me go." He was stunned by that. It was beyond his ability at first to grasp that there might be a time for his wife to die, as well as a time to live, and that a dying person might actually have some sense of when that moment might arrive. But that was exactly what she was saying. "My time has come and you need to let me go."

As we sat *watching* this powerful scene, Debbie, who all along had been fully engaged auditorially, began to make a bewailing noise, the kind she would make when she wanted me to know she needed to communicate something important. She was telling me that she identified with what was being said on the screen. At first I was not paying attention to her, since the film was so vivid. I thought at first that she was just appreciating the pathos of the movie. But when I looked at her, tears were streaming down her cheeks and she began to moan intensely.

I hit the pause button on the remote and turned my attention to my captivated bride. I was choked up from listening to the conversation between the great author and his dying wife. But knowing Debbie as I did, I recognized that this was more than her just being emotional over a film. She rarely cried watching a movie, even those that were quite moving. This was something significant, something really important that she was trying to communicate to me.

Things were quiet for a while in the room where we sat. I sensed a kind of heaviness in the air, as if something was about to be communicated that I knew I did not want to hear. It was about to be "said," though, and there was nothing I could do about it. It was like the moment before a judge reads a verdict to a defendant, a defendant whose lawyer has already told him that things may not go well with the jury. It is like a moment that stretches out seemingly endlessly, as if time itself was moving in slow motion, and yet you know that a fateful thing is about to take place. And that thing, that word, once spoken, will change everything else for the rest of your life. It can never be taken back. The time dragged on ponderously for those few brief moments when I just knew I was about to face such a life-changing event.

"What, Babe?" I asked. "What is going on?"

She groaned. "I need to tell you something," she was saying to me in the only way she could. I did not want to ask the question. I now began to suspect what the answer was going to be, and so I did not want to continue this communication. I needed to catch up. I also wanted to have this conversation at another time, if ever. But she was not to be put off. She passionately continued struggling to communicate.

Reluctantly, I posed the question to Debbie. "Honey, are you trying to tell me that *you* want *me* to let *you* go?" Her countenance was profoundly serious as she cracked a bit of a smile.

That was exactly what she was trying to say to me. It was clear there was a kind of happiness and contentment in her demeanor, as if it was something she had wanted to say for a long time. Now it was *said*. This "word" to me had been lurking in her heart for some time and the words of Joy to her husband "Jack" Lewis were simply the catalyst that ignited the spark. Something in her heart was set free. And yet, there was a great soberness in that moment for both of us. This was a very powerful moment in our lives. We had crossed a kind of Rubicon together, but it was yet to be seen how it would play out. I still needed some time to catch up and to figure out what had just happened.

Debbie had been thinking a lot about heaven in the months before we had this "talk." I had been coaching her to trust God to give her many more years of happiness here. She was now taking issue with the coach. I wanted her on earth; her heart was turned upward. Perhaps she had already wanted to say this, but had not come to a place of being convinced that the Lord was bringing her to her final days. Now she was sure. Solemn and stunned, I went into the other room in order to better process what my wife just told me. I needed to be alone for a few minutes so she could not feel the apprehension in my body language or hear it in my voice. Maybe when I came back to the room in a few minutes she would have changed her mind, thought better of it, or had some doubts about what she was really thinking.

But when I walked back into the room, there she sat, with that same look of excited inquiry on her face. I mustered up the emotional fortitude to ask "Are you sure you want me to let you go?" I tearfully appealed to her, with a sense of both resistance and at the same time almost of peculiar relief. I knew if she were to depart from this world it would mean her freedom from this seemingly endless suffering and pain endured all these years. So, for her sake, how could I not let go?

It would also mean freedom for me. But that realization was immediately followed by a sense of guilt. Bittersweet emotions began to flow thru my inner being. Is feeling relieved wrong? Do I need to somehow hide this feeling? That was always one thought in my mind, as it probably is in the minds of most families of desperately ill people. Do you pray for more years in this life, or for release from the suffering?

"Sweetheart, do you think that the Lord is going to take you soon?" Immediately she blinked. "Yes, I am sure."

I paused a long while and gathered composure and then asked her, "Do you have a sense how much longer you will live?"

She blinked with a big groan. The blink meant yes. I took the groan to mean, "Not long," but I was uncertain just what that meant.

"Do you think longer than two years?"

No.

I then asked her, "One year?"

No.

I continued to probe her until I finally inquired, "Two months?"

At that point her response was an emphatic blink, which I knew meant "yes." This answer was far more than I was ready to cope with.

I cannot adequately express how I felt in those dark moments just before Christmas. My wife knew she would die soon. I was not in a state of despair, but I was filled with sadness and sorrow at the loss that was looming ever larger on my horizon. I don't want to be guilty of claiming to know something more about God than is found in the Bible, but I felt at the time that I knew something of the anguished heart of our heavenly Father as he was giving his Son over to death. Yet, in some other way like the Father, I knew that the "end" was not really the "End." At the same time it was beginning to feel like it was the end for me.

I looked down at her beautiful face. It was etched with a clear and palpable expectation and excitement. It was also marked with the weary signs of long years dealing with pain, seizures, disappointments, and frustration. She was happy and tired at one and the same time. Her countenance betrayed all of what she was feeling at the time—love for me and for God, anticipation at what she believed what was about to happen in her struggle with illness, and weariness in the battle with the great enemy we had faced for so long. She did not need to speak. I knew her so well by this time I could read her body language, the look on her face, the quiver of her lip, the twitching in her face. I was at peace with the way God was preparing her for what was to come.

The End Approaches

It seemed as if Debbie actually knew how much longer the Lord was going to give her, as she knew her health situation had been rapidly deteriorating over the previous weeks, ever since our return from the vacation. She undoubtedly could tell within herself that the end was coming and coming soon. The speeding train was about to hit the wall. Debbie's decline was not at first this obvious to the rest of us who were part of her life, since her condition was so bad in the first place. But it was obvious to her, and within a couple of short weeks after we watched *Shadowlands* together it would be obvious to me, her mother, and to everyone else who knew her.

For almost seventeen years now we had battled this enemy. We had used every weapon in our arsenal. We hung on when the various emergencies came along. We employed all of the technology available to us in fighting the good fight. We kept our spirits high through the whole process, praying for each other and facing each day, even the depressing ones, with the expectation that, whatever happened, God would be glorified and we would be blessed. We "high-fived" each other, even if only symbolically, when we won victories, though most of them were small victories to be sure. We wept together in those moments when despair seemed a breath away, but we wept *together*, and that made all the difference. Now the thought of separation from my soul mate became the ultimate challenge at hand.

Our oneness in Christ was never more real than the day Debbie told me I had to let her go. Since we were one, it meant that my very soul was about to be ripped apart. It was almost as if we had been engaged in a seventeen-year-long tennis doubles' match. Debbie and I were on one side of the net, while our opponents, illness and despair, faced us on the other side. At times it was not clear whether the greatest opponent was the illness itself or the despair that loomed large after we'd win small victories. Of course, tennis matches are exciting to watch from the sidelines. The difference was that we were not spectators in this game, and this game was a match to the death. But we played our hearts out and did not give in to the darkness taking shape around us.

Many times during those years it would have been tempting to give up. There were people in our lives who wondered why we fought so hard against the inevitable. They were right about the inevitability part. Within a few years of my wife's contracting MS, it became painfully obvious there would be no reversal, no "cure," and, apparently, no divine intervention for healing. It is not that we gave up on the *possibility* God would heal Debbie, it was just more and more clear that this did not seem to be God's will for us. Our work with Joni and with other disabled people also demonstrated that there are many for whom God's will does not include immediate divine healing in this life. In spite of that, we had not given up, nor had we even considered the increasingly popular, and in our view wrong, idea of assisted suicide.

Euthanasia, so called "mercy death," has become an extremely controversial issue in the modern world, and the more so in the last few decades. Jack Kevorkian, the "doctor of death," made assisted suicide a front page issue in the final years of Debbie's life. In 1991 Derek Humphrey published the book, *Final Exit*. He was a major figure in the Hemlock Society, an organization dedicated to the idea that people, especially terminally ill or severely disabled people, ought to have the right to end their lives if they wish. Humphrey's idea was not a new one—the Euthanasia Society of America was formed in 1938. But public opinion was generally against euthanasia until recently. Then the late twentieth century witnessed a series of high-profile cases of handicapped people or their families taking charge of ending their own lives.

People who are extraordinarily challenged, seriously ill, or severely disabled have painful and complex lives, lives often lived at the very edge of despair and desperation. Some of them find themselves sympathetic with the modern German philosopher Karl Jaspers, who argued that the only real philosophical problem to solve in our time is why people should not commit suicide. Jaspers was actually talking about all people, including very healthy people. Imagine how much more intensely this question is faced by the suffering and terminally ill.

In spite of the fact that Debbie's disease seemed to be moving her inevitably toward death at a young age, we never saw euthanasia as an option, even when the doctors essentially told us that there was no hope. There were many reasons it was not the answer.* For one thing, *life is a gift from God.* Job said, "Naked I came from my mother's womb, and naked I will depart. The LORD gave and the LORD has taken away; may the name of the LORD be praised" (1:21). The giving and the taking of life lies in the hands of God, and it would be the height of presumption for us to preempt God in making decisions to end life. The teaching in the Bible was clear to us.

Another reason was that we both believed that God placed us here to glorify him and to serve *others.* Severely disabled and terminally ill people often make a huge impact on the lives of those around them. This is even true of ill people with great difficulty in communicating, such as my wife. I have already recounted some of the ways God used Debbie to change the lives of people around her for the better. It is perfectly normal for suffering people to want to end their suffering. But it is important for them and for their loved ones to understand they have been placed here by God for a purpose, and while God did not directly cause their problem, he can use it to impact others for their own benefit as well as the Kingdom of God. We knew that. We saw it happening in our circle of friends and family, and in the ministry to the disabled that God gave us.

Christian people know that physical illness is not simply a battle over biology. There is an added dimension that Scripture calls *spiritual warfare.* We do not wage war only against physical "flesh and blood," but against "spiritual forces of evil" (2 Corinthians 10:3–6; Ephesians 6:10–20). Scripture teaches that the Devil is the one holding the power of death (Hebrews 2:14). This probably refers to the fact that death entered the world when Satan tempted Adam and Eve to sin and they yielded to the temptation. This means Satan is the father of death, and he also holds the fear of death over us (Hebrews 2:15).

---

* For a discussion of reasons why not to employ mercy killing or doctor assisted euthanasia, see, for instance, Scott B. Rae, *Moral Choices: An Introduction to Ethics;* John S. Feinberg and Paul D. Feinberg, *Ethics for a Brave New World;* or Joni Eareckson Tada, *When Is it Right to Die?*

Even if Satan wants all people dead, this does not mean he causes all deaths. God is sovereign over the Devil and it is God, as we have already seen, who is the Lord of life and death. But it is true that Satan loves death. He revels in it and inflicts damage on God's good world through it. There is a sense in which behind every tragic death the Devil is present. Behind every young mother snatched from her children by a drunk driver, every teenager whose body is ravaged by a deadly overdose of drugs, behind these things and others lurks a malignant force that finds it a thing to cherish when people perish.

The Enemy calls us to come to him and die, even as Christ calls us to come to him and live. Satan tempts the suffering person and the terminally ill to despair, to lose all hope. Part of that temptation in some cases is to "escape" through euthanasia. But to do so would be to give in to the chaos, essentially to concede that the Enemy has won. This is simply not an option for followers of Jesus Christ.

My life with Debbie was often marked by spiritual warfare. We had to regularly dress in the protective spiritual armor of Christ to withstand the attacks of the Enemy. Ephesians 6:16 and 17 tell us that the armor includes the shield of faith, the helmet of our salvation, and the Word of God, which is our offensive weapon to counter the Enemy after fending off his attacks. Access to the full armor of Christ is another reason to believe that suffering people can most fully engage and endure their suffering only when Christ is present in their lives. One cannot defeat Satan without, in the words of Martin Luther, the Right Man on our side.

Still yet another reason for not yielding to the temptation of physician-assisted suicide is that God uses our struggles to conform us into the *image of Christ*. If we believe God to be a sovereign God, then we will know that nothing happens to us without his permission. In addition, we will know that nothing happens to *us* that does not also happen *for* us. Whatever comes into our lives often can be for our own good, if we will trust God for it to be so. It seems that gratuitous evil, which is seemingly purposeless, is a very difficult subject even for theologians to resolve. But the fact that there is no final intellectual resolution does not mean we cannot resolve this in our relationship to God. We learn to trust him through it all.

It is also clear, however, that God as a loving Father also holds us *accountable* for our actions and choices. It is not that he is a stern and autocratic judge. If you are a parent you know that loving a child also means expecting them to live up to their potential and setting consequences if they behave in less than honorable ways.

Scripture teaches that we will all appear before the judgment seat of Christ to be judged for the deeds we do in life (2 Corinthians 5:1–10). Debbie and I wanted our choices to please God and we wanted to make decisions that would glorify him. In fact, as time went by, our mind-set shifted more from anger to wanting to love him above all else. I think many people progress through stages of the Christian experience. At one level they live their lives thinking they just don't want God to be *displeased* with them. But at some other point, Christians maturing in their faith get to the place where the primary motivation is that they want God to be *pleased* with their lives. That is a sign of real progress.

Ready for Heaven

The nature of Debbie's illness was now about to change. She had fought a long and hard battle, but she was no longer so certain she had any will or capacity to use Herculean efforts to fight anymore. Joni Eareckson Tada had a book out at the time, *When Is It Right to Die?* There is a place in Joni's volume where she says that dying begins when "a person rapidly and irreversibly deteriorates, a person for whom death is imminent, a person who is beyond reasonable hope of recovery." My wife knew that this was approaching in her own body, and in addition to knowing this, there was a second thing going on in her heart. She knew she was *ready for heaven*, and Debbie had an uncanny conviction that God was calling her home.

How do you know when you are ready to die? The most basic issue is assurance you belong to Christ, because anyone who understands Scripture will see that knowing Christ is the most important factor in life. For facing death with complete confidence, we have to know the One who faced death, to pay the price for our sins, and conquered it through his resurrection. Being at peace with God is crucial since Christ is the source of life and hope even for the dying person.

How do you know for certain you belong to Christ? The Bible answers that question in several different ways, but in Romans 8:15-16, the apostle Paul lists one of the most important reasons. He says that

Christians have received the Spirit of adoption which causes them to recognize God as their "Abba, Father." Paul then states that the Holy Spirit bears witness with our spirit that we are the children of God and heirs to God's Kingdom. What that means is that the indwelling Spirit confirms to us that God is our close heavenly Father. In theological terms, God is both *immanent* and *transcendent*. For the Christian, God is not merely a distant deity. He is not "the Man Upstairs" or some other unfamiliar entity. God is *Papa*, "Father," even "Daddy" to the Christian. The Spirit himself makes that relationship real in our lives, so we know with our spirit we are heirs of God and co-heirs with Christ.

Another way of saying this is that assurance comes with faith. When someone believes in Jesus for salvation, that act of faith brings a confidence or a pledge along with it. By looking away from ourselves to Christ, we know this very act of faith and trust makes salvation real to us. What people need as they begin to face death is assurance about their relationship with God. That assurance comes with faith.

How do you know you are ready to die? For many, there is the need to know that our lives have counted for something. Not many achieve such monumental accomplishments as to become famous in this world. But it is important to know we have accomplished something, that we have made a difference in the lives of people, and that we have left some piece of ourselves behind to live on in the experience of others.

When we are facing imminent death, we want to know that the ones closest to us are prepared to face the hour with us. We hope they can be there for us, but even more that they are ready to deal with the issues facing them as they watch us quietly slipping away into, as Hamlet says, that "country from whose bourn no traveler returns." This isn't always possible, of course, because the way other people cope with death can't be controlled. But we'd like to know we don't leave loved ones destitute or in despair over our loss.

Debbie had all of these things on her side. She knew she knew the Lord. She had been certain of that for a long time, and she spent many sweet hours in prayer, speaking to the Lord and sensing his replies. She had no fear of the grave. She could look into its jaws with no apprehension whatsoever since her faith in Christ was strong. Debbie also knew that her life had counted. Though she would have downplayed the extent to which she impacted people, she knew we had reached the arms of ministry and service out to many people in our disability ministry. I am quite certain Debbie never really understood how many people she had blessed, but she had no reason in the world to feel her life had been wasted. She also knew she was leaving me in good shape. The Lord had prepared me for this hour for many years. She also knew I would continue being helped by many, many wonderful people who shared in our life and ministry together.

As Christmas came and went, Debbie communicated that she wanted to leave her life in the hands of the Lord and not continue all of the extreme efforts to keep her functioning. She had been having increasingly difficult time breathing and so finally we had to face the question of a ventilator. This meant her permanent attachment to artificial respiration, yet another of those difficult decisions terminally ill and severely handicapped people have to face. Technology gives us some great new possibilities for extending life, but it is not always clear that we ought to use every technology possible. In their book *Ethics for a Brave New World*, John and Paul Feinberg, two evangelical Christian ethicists, say that on using certain procedures, "if it is unclear that the medical procedure would improve the patient's condition, and it might harm him instead, there is no moral obligation to undertake the new treatment."

I have to be honest. I was having a very difficult time dealing with Debbie's intuition both that her body was shutting down and that God was calling her home. It was hard for me to process the concept of her wanting me to let her go. I thought, if this was true, why couldn't I feel it or see it the way Debbie did? I struggled with this feeling for days. In the film *We Were Soldiers*, Mel Gibson portrayed an army captain pledged to carry out his duty faithfully, only to witness most of his men killed in action. "They lived out my promise," he sadly noted. I felt the same way. It is difficult even now for me to relive those days of anguish and uncertainty. I realized that my dear wife was more spiritual than I was, but I still could not understand how she could be so certain God was going to bring her to himself within such a specific time frame as "two months."

How would a person know that? I talked it over with her mother, Florence. Debbie indicated to her mother that she knew her time had come and that she did not want to fight any more. Florence was very quiet. She later told me she knew it would be hard, but she wanted to recognize that Debbie was a spiritual woman who knew her path. This was a somber season, without a doubt. I still was not yet ready to concede defeat. Of course, Debbie did not think of it as "defeat," but instead as a final victory. She was going to win against the illness, but not in the way I would have preferred or expected.

For two weeks I prayed and processed Debbie's wishes in my mind and spirit and discussed with friends and advisors her readiness to die. During this same time I was in meetings trying to deal with the fracturing of our church and a slowly recovering business.

These were hard days. Everything was upside-down. I had to find a way to understand what was happening and to gain peace in my heart—peace in being willing to let her go, and peace this was the path the will of God was taking us. So, I wrote this emotional letter to my wife at Christmas time. With her mother at her side, I could barely get the words out to read it to her:

December 1995

The Gift of My Heart Thoughts

Sweetest,

My Beeba, you know how I love you. You know my care. You know all that has been weighing on me. Much with the church, much with my business, and much as I tire seeing you suffer.

You're such an inspiration to me and so many others. You are so special to me; not the same girl I married. Not only has our gracious God transformed you but through you he has transformed me as I've seen his light most often through you. Above all for that I thank you!

I've never doubted your love for me and as you've seen God change my heart, I know you've not doubted mine for you. You're beautiful outside but even more beautiful inside. It excites my heart as I consider you glorified in Christ in eternity—even more

---

beautiful! A new body, a new mind and a new heart. No more suffering, sin or depravity.

Joni's book on heaven is exciting me for you (and me). Especially as I see you yearn to be with him for ever.

Back a while I had real concerns down deep that your faith was emotionally based. Did you really embrace all that God had for you? Now I see your faith strong and unwavering. My expectations have been exceeded--God often seems to work that way in my life. In many ways I cherish you--as the best wife a man could have.

As you often told me, you didn't want any part of a hospital--particularly a respirator or life support. I've resisted that for many years--and told you how I couldn't live without you (not like in the beginning). God has now impressed me with the need to let go as he may call you home. In a way that's most difficult--and yet I sense that in a more permanent way it's most fulfilling.

Debbie, my Pumpkin-ninka, for me to know you are so confident really excites me more than saddens me. As you've responded to the book on heaven by Joni I'm convinced, clearly you are ready.

This Christmas, my sweetheart, my gift is to release you to him in his time. I yearn with you. I look heavenward and share your joy. Be free to yield to his release of suffering, my Babe. Things will be different, very different; positively different. I yearn to be there with you, my sweetheart. We are foreigners in this land--heaven is our "real home."

I know how you love the home I prepared for you--but Jesus has prepared a better place for each of us. I praise him with you for that and look towards our eternal home. We are homeward bound, my Sweetest, and I thank you for your example of faith! God has used you so profoundly in my walk with him––I thank you! Many nights and days I've watched you, years ago in ice blankets and lonely New York hospital rooms and more recently choking and struggling to breathe. Thank you, my Beeba, for fighting and being here for me––but thank you more for fighting the good fight for Him. You've run the race. I'm not sure, of course, of God's time but I've come to a place in my heart of peace that God is preparing me to be without you. I know you share that confidence and trust him with me. You know, sweetest, the very special place you'll have in my heart forever.

I will always thank God in every remembrance of you, my love, my sweetest, my precious Beeba.

This Christmas I yield to be separated from you, in God's time––but only for a short time with confidence and hope––a positive hope of dwelling in his presence with you forever and ever.

Love,

Mark

P.S. So many years now you've been unable to move, speak and see. You have persevered a most incredible trial. Blessed is the one who perseveres under trial because when he has stood the test he will receive the crown of life (James 1:12).

Within hours, we would be celebrating the birth of the Christ, the one who gave us the reason to know that Debbie's jar of clay would soon be changed into an incorruptible vessel. With the writing and reading of this letter, I finally had peace of heart about letting my bride go to meet her heavenly Bridegroom.

Debbie's Blessing

Becky and I had been molded into a relationship of friendship in the firing kiln of Debbie's ordeal. I felt after a time much like a big brother to her, and then later, I felt a deepening and developing of affection for her that could become dangerous. I continued to pray and to ask a close friend and spiritual brother to hold me accountable to him and to God as I walked through those dark days. My focus was ministry to my wife, and Becky's focus, likewise, was ministry to Debbie.

Becky was not with us in December, 1995 during those precious and intense days. But I knew that if Debbie was correct, she would soon shrug off her mortal coil, and some day, in the not-too-distant future, Becky and I might find our paths joining together. I must say this became a perplexing time for me, indeed. I loved my wife as deeply as I possibly could. Yet it was because of my love for her that I felt compelled to speak to her about Becky. Debbie and I were one, and I believed that it would have been wrong of me to conceal from her what I thought might happen at some point after she went to be with Christ. But of course, here is a dilemma—how do you talk to your dying wife about your notion of marrying someone else after she was gone?

Some might even consider this a bizarre situation. Granted, it certainly was unique. This state of affairs was a real "God thing," something I could not have predicted or planned. I was not looking for someone else to replace Debbie. But the fact was that my wife was dying, and it appeared her death might be only weeks away. Who knew how much longer she'd even be conscious?

After much prayer I decided to talk to Debbie about Becky. I felt compelled to do so out of love for my dear lady. How could I not? And so with a peculiar peace in my heart as I approached my lover we broke down in a release of emotions, anticipating our seemingly imminent separation. I embraced my beloved wife. We cried. And we cried. The emotional pain then seemed to subside. We regained our composure, squarely facing the reality that death would soon part us. It was a bitter moment in many ways, and yet also a moment of joy and release. For the first time in a long time we were facing something completely new.

Then, at the right moment, I asked her what would probably be the last but also the most sensitive question I would ever ask: "How would you feel—if. . ." Long pause. "If when God takes you home, I pursued a relationship with Becky?"

The stakes were high. But I felt somehow safe in asking her. Perhaps it was because I knew we were one both in marriage and in the Spirit, and I had no fear I had somehow underestimated her character or discernment. And, as I expected, she was not hurt at all. There was no miscommunication. She was very alert and she made a very clear and distinct blink. "Yes!" A tear ran down her face, and her beautiful features were creased with a smile. I was looking at the face of a woman transformed into the loving and selfless image of Christ.

Surely, Debbie must have considered that she had the special opportunity of getting to know the person who would later be at the center of her husband's life. I later learned, that previously Becky had hinted a request to Debbie that someday she would want her to be her maid of honor, if she ever were to get married. Well now that seemed sure not to happen that way. That was simply not an issue. I sensed that Debbie felt profoundly honored by my telling her of the prospect of Becky and me being together. Words are simply inadequate to describe the moment. Wow. God was in this in a powerful way!

As if this weren't enough already, I then took another presumptuous, maybe faithful, leap in the midst of the emotion of it all. I said to Debbie that whatever happens it would be my heart's desire, should I ever be blessed with a daughter, to name her *Debbie*. I sensed then, and I sense even more now, she felt peace in knowing that my life would likely somehow go on joyfully and happily after she was gone. Knowing that her favorite person in the world outside her family might be my new wife in the years ahead brought Debbie great satisfaction and peace, both of which were very easily evident on her face. Oh, how this spoke once again of the selfless character molded in her person by the Master Potter! She was more concerned about my future than about her own impending death.

I was reminded of the time I asked her years before if I might go on a ski trip to Switzerland. I had felt guilty, yet her selfless response freed me. It freed me to enjoy my trip, but even more importantly, it freed me to love and respect her more deeply.

When Debbie gave her blessing, my heart was on the verge of breaking, both for sadness and joy. But the darkest days were just ahead.

Chapter 13

Crumbling of the Jar

—§§

A Time of Preparation

THERE WAS A sacred intensity to the little time we knew was left. Despite the emotional weight of our circumstances, Debbie and I had a very special and meaningful time during the holidays. We did a lot of one-on-one sharing, praying and reminiscing, even though communication was way more difficult than it had ever been. I tried to prepare for the mental and emotional ordeal I knew was coming soon.

Just how does one cope with the knowledge that a loved one is about to die, especially when that loved one is your beloved wife, a woman not even yet middle-aged? Do you try having a "stiff upper lip"? Do you "get your act together"? Do you just "let go and let God"? All of the standard lines and pat clichés can never really assist you when the time comes to face the inevitable. And so I purposed to cherish these sacred hours with her.

In early January we talked to her doctors about what was going on in Debbie's body. My bride's body was in a clear state of final decline. One clear sign was that she lost her ability to show feelings on her face. This was a bitter blow. Even when Debbie lost her ability to speak, she could still communicate to others what she was feeling and thinking by her facial expressions. Thousands of times over the years I felt her love for me when her face would glow with affection. On uncounted occasions I knew whether she was in pain, whether she felt contented, whether she was filled with joy or consumed with worry, by simply glancing at her demeanor.

Even as blind people often find their other senses enhanced to make up for their lack of eyesight, so I had learned to receive communication from my dear wife in ways beyond the verbal. A look, the twitch of her eyebrows, the movements of her lips or the tilt of her head often communicated volumes in an instant. Now not even these small abilities were possible for her, and my heart was breaking inside me.

More than all of that, Debbie's smile which had lightened a thousand hearts over the years was now gone. Her genuine smile had been so uplifting to so many people. In the 1988 Olympics in Seoul, South Korea, the South Korean government made smiling a national decree for its citizens. One wonders how many of those smiles were manufactured for the cameras and the television audience. Have you heard of the "Pan American Smile"? This refers to the smile of the flight attendant as he or she waves "bye, bye" to you as you exit the plane, a smile whose genuineness is often suspect.

Not so with Debbie. Throughout the years her arresting and intoxicating smile often creased her countenance with marks of joy and enthusiasm. Though many would say she had little reason to smile, still her smile was frequent, broad, and genuine. Her facial demonstration of joy and contentment was a ministry in itself. But now the ravages of the hated disease were taking that away from her, not because she no longer smiled within, but because her facial muscles had been frozen by the MS. Still, God was good and gracious to us in those increasingly difficult weeks in early 1996. We were both smiling inside, but that smile was not evident on either of our faces.

It shortly became clear to me that what Debbie had previously known and communicated was becoming a present reality. She also knew, even more clearly than she did just a few weeks ago, that her health was now worse than it had ever been, and her body was shutting down. I knew what was coming, and I did not want her to go. For sixteen years my prayer was that Debbie might be restored. Though I had learned to live with what appeared to be God's answer to that prayer—"No"—I never quite gave up praying for her healing. Selfishly, I realized that even if I remarried my life simply would never be the same. Even with the evidence of Debbie's demise in front of my very eyes, part of me was still not willing to give up. But that faded quickly as the days went by.

Certainly in another sense I knew when Debbie was gone the difficulty of caring for an invalid would be over. That care-giving task had been a long and heavy load, and the more so as she increasingly lost control of her faculties and bodily functions. Debbie was never really a burden to me, of course, at least not since I came to know the Lord. Life with Debbie was certainly a challenge, but not, overall, a burden. I had learned to adapt to that challenge, and so caring for my wife was simply part of life.

I had taken it in stride, the way other men know that part of their job as a husband is mowing the lawn or raking leaves in autumn. It was part of loving my wife with all my heart. As husbands we are admonished to love our wives as Christ loves the church. Christians are to be good stewards of the circumstances God places in our path. It does no good to wish for different ones. Contentment is a very important quality, and it is found only when we act as passionate caretakers of the lives we actually have, not the ones we wish we could have.

But it was certain that the time upon us was a new kind of challenge. If I could love her with all my heart how could I not also release her? If she was right that God was calling her home, then would I not have to face that, even as I had faced the challenge of caring for her during the past years? I knew God was calling her, but I also knew I was going to miss my lady. She was still my darling, and she was so beautiful to me.

I saw Debbie's broken and twisted body now in a near fetal position before me. But at the same time I saw two other visions in my mind's eye. I saw the Debbie I married, the woman who was stunningly lovely, and with whom I had shared a wonderful honeymoon and early marriage. Her face still shone in my vision with the joy she expressed when we renovated that first house together. Beyond the shattering clay lying on that bed I perceived the woman God gave me to be my bride.

The other vision that came to mind was the Debbie God would one day raise from the dead and grant a glorified body that is incorruptible, spiritual, and raised in power (1 Corinthians 15:42–44). Resurrection from the dead into a body that is perfect is the biblical view of the future of believers. There she would be able to run and laugh once again, and look at the world around her with those beautiful eyes. She will even dance! One of Debbie's favorite songs was "Joni's Waltz," which expresses this hope so well. That was the Debbie I could see by faith through the bitter mist that began to sting my eyes as I contemplated the difficult days and weeks ahead of us.

We had great "talks" in those last weeks. To this day I thank God for his timing in having allowed us to be so prepared! Our conversations were extremely focused, since we both knew our time together was short. In classical mythology there is a story about a man named Damocles, a courtier in attendance at the court of Dionysius. He so persistently praised the power and glory of Dionysius that the tyrant, in order to show the precariousness of rank and power, gave a banquet and had a sword suspended above the head of Damocles by a single hair. The expression "the sword of Damocles" has come to signify one who faces an ever-present peril. That was the kind of peril looming large in our life in January, 1996. That was our clear and present peril.

Yet, it is probably not exactly accurate to call it "peril." Certainly the perilous situation existed, and it was becoming obvious it meant that death was near. Certainly there was no escape. But even more so we were convinced that this death was simply the path to a greater glory! Paul tells us that nothing, not even death, can separate us from the love of God that is in Christ Jesus our Lord (Romans 8:38–39). He also says believers, live to the Lord, and if we die, we die to the Lord (Romans 14:8). Whether we live or die, we belong to the Lord, and even at death we resign ourselves to the Father's will and try pleasing him in the way we die.

The apostle Paul also notes that at the time of the second coming of Christ, the "dead in Christ" will rise first (1 Thessalonians 4:16). What an interesting phrase, the "dead in Christ"! In spite of their death, believers who die are still united to Christ. But that does not mean real death is not a reality; it certainly is. We control neither life nor death, and God is in charge of both. "The Lord gave and the Lord has taken away. Blessed be the name of the Lord" (Job 1:21).

Living to Die and Dying to Live

Scripture says a lot about death. In the first and final analysis, death is both directly and indirectly related to human sin. Adam was given the possibility that he and his offspring would not face death if he would only obey God's command. If on the other hand he disobeyed God and ate from the tree of the knowledge of good and evil, he would certainly face death (Genesis 2:16-17). God said in the day Adam ate from the tree he would surely die.

Adam did not die physically on the day he ate the fruit, and there is good reason to believe the phrase "on the day you eat from it" is a Hebrew way of saying, "know this for certain" (see 1 Kings 2:37 for a similar usage). Because he ate the fruit, his physical death, and the death of all of his offspring, became inevitable. But Adam also lost something else that was very vital on the day he and Eve ate of the fruit. Together with his wife, he lost his innocence, his simple trust in God, and unimpeded access to the Father. A death took place on the day of that first sin, but it was a spiritual death, not a physical one.

Adam would certainly die because of his disobedience, but not Adam alone. "Therefore, just as sin entered the world through one man, and death through sin, in this way death spread to all men, because all sinned" (Romans 5:12). History exonerates this verse of Scripture since no one who has ever lived has escaped passing through the valley of the shadow of death.

But that is not the end of it. While death is a certainty for all persons, it is not the same for all persons. Christian believers can face the hour of death with confidence and without fear. They can know when they stand before the great and final Judge they do not have to fear condemnation, for there is "no condemnation for those who are in Christ Jesus" (Romans 8:1). Still, in more than one sense death really stinks because it amputates a limb of the life of the one left behind.

Some skeptics assert they do not believe there is any kind of final judgment, that death is the final state of reality and there is no conscious life after death. Interestingly, though, even some of the greatest critics of traditional Christianity, and traditional religion in general, have had a difficult time convincing themselves that this life is all there is. For this reason, even some critics of biblical Christianity argue there must be some kind of final judgment.

Immanuel Kant, in many ways the godfather of modern liberal theology, is a case in point. Kant argued there must be a conscious life after death and a final judgment before a just God. He contended that in this life there often is an inadequate distribution of justice. The wicked in many cases are not punished for the damage they have done to others, and the righteous in many cases are not rewarded for the good they have done for the world. Inequalities abound in this life. There must, therefore, be a just assessment in some venue, and if these people die without justice that reward or punishment must be distributed in the afterlife. Kant had little sympathy for traditional views about the Bible or even Christ, but he was convinced that there must be a righteous God who would judge all humans for deeds done in their lifetime, whether good or evil.

Kant was probably onto something, for the very nature of justice demands an afterlife. But Christians have an even more sure hope—the testimony of the Bible and the example of the resurrection of Jesus. Beyond even this, Christians can be confident to face that passage to eternity with assurance that Jesus will bear them safely to the other side. What faces Christians is no "grim reaper," but a triumphant and resurrected Savior. Because of that, they can face the hour of death without terror.

There are other things Christians understand about death. One is that it is the terminal outcome of living in a fallen world. In 1 Corinthians 15:26 the apostle Paul tells us the last enemy to be abolished is *death*. That means the final death of death itself is still in the future. All persons, including Christians, will walk through the valley of the shadow of death and will even face that moment themselves where they draw their final breath in this age. Christians live in the "already, but not yet" of salvation. We experience the kingdom of God now, but the full and final benefits of that salvation will not be fully realized until the new age dawns. For the Christian eternal life begins now. We begin to experience it in this age of our existence, but the full glory of it still awaits the time after we pass out of this life.

We also know that we will leave our sin and its ill effects behind once and for all when we die. Even the best of us still find ourselves failing to live up to the ideal all of the time and still acting in ways that are, to one degree or another, destructive toward ourselves and others. Hebrews 12:23 states that believers have come to Mt. Zion, "to the assembly of the firstborn whose names have been written in heaven, to God who is the judge of all, to the spirits of righteous people made perfect." Those in heaven are the spirits of righteous people made perfect. Complete perfection, that is, the elimination of all sin, is never accomplished in this life, but it is a gift from God to those who have died and gone to be with him. In many ways this may be the greatest of all the blessings of "dying in Christ" since sin is such a destructive force in this life.

Death for the believer is also an entering into eternal life. Once death was a curse, but now it is a blessing. It is not a *payment for* sin but a final *dying to* sin. Dietrich Bonhoeffer was a Christian pastor martyred by the Nazi Gestapo in April, 1945. In his book *Letters and Papers from Prison*, he described death as the "supreme festival on the road to freedom." Pastor Bonhoeffer had plenty of time to think about death in the concentration camp at Flossenburg, so his testimony bears a great deal of weight.

Strikingly, almost unbelievably, the Bible actually calls dying "gain" (Philippians 1:21), a gain ushering us into the very presence of the Lord (2 Corinthians 5:1-8). The non-Christian world has often has a different perspective. In his *Nicomachean Ethics*, Aristotle stated that death "appears to be the end of everything." In *Being and Nothingness* Jean-Paul Sartre contended that death "removes all meaning from life." An epitaph on the tomb of a Roman pagan from the ancient world has three simple words inscribed on it: "Gone, gone, gone." Christians, on the other hand, have a "blessed hope" (Titus 2:13), and live ultimately not for this age but for the age to come (John 12:25). As A. W. Tozer reminded us, "we are made for eternity as well as for time."

So, what happens at death? Paul says that to die is to "depart and be with Christ" (Philippians 1:23), which is far better than remaining in the flesh. To be "absent from the body" is to be "present with the Lord" (2 Corinthians 5:8). The Psalmist noted, "My flesh and my heart may fail, but God is the strength of my heart and my portion forever"

(Psalm 73:26). When the evangelist Stephen in the New Testament was about to die he saw the Lord in heaven waiting to receive him (Acts 7:54–60). He asked God to forgive those about to stone him, and then he said, "Lord Jesus, receive my spirit."

This idea of death being gain is displayed in John Bunyan's classic allegorical explanation of the Christian life, *Pilgrim's Progress*, where the passage through the River of Death leads immediately to the Heavenly City. The Christian has this major hope, that death is the immediate portal to the blessedness of being in the very presence of God. Death is not to be feared, but, in the timing of God's purposes in our lives, it is a day to be embraced. It is the route to a true knowledge of God, whom we will finally see "face to face" (1 Corinthians 13:12). In other words, death, and what lies beyond death, is the final goal of life. It does not make life meaningless; instead, in a real sense, it is what makes life meaningful.

Debbie understood these things. She spent many years thinking about them, increasingly knowing that her disease would likely be the instrument to usher her into the age to come. She understood that Christ in his death destroyed "him who had the power of death, the Devil" (Hebrews 2:14). That meant she did not have to fear death (Hebrews 2:15). It also meant that death was not a mystery to her or to me. Shakespeare's Prince Hamlet thought of suicide, but feared the outcome since he did not know the nature of existence beyond the grave:

> "To die, to sleep, to sleep! Perchance to dream—ay,
> there's the rub. For in that sleep of death what dreams
> may come, when we have shuffled off this mortal coil
> must give us pause. . . . But that dread of something
> after death—that undiscovered country, from whose bourn
> no traveler returns—puzzles the will, and makes us
> rather bear those ills we have, than to fly to others
> that we know not of?"

Debbie did not share the puzzlement of the Danish prince about what lay on the other side of death, for she was not filled with doubts. She knew, and I did also, that Christ was waiting for her, and that he would welcome her to an eternity free from pain and suffering. She knew the Lord who is known in the Bible as the Alpha and Omega, the first and the last, the one who was before all things and who also holds the end of life and the end of history in his hands (Revelation 1:17-18).

Debbie's face was always placid and serene when we discussed the fact that the MS might one day take her life. Her tender and delicate heart was filled with rock-ribbed certainty when she contemplated the open mouth of the grave. Now her face was fixed and frozen by the illness, but her heart was filled with the same confidence in God that she had known these many years. Whenever we would speak of heaven in those last days her face would glow. She was like a runner coming to the end of a race. Seeing the finish line before her, she summoned all her final strength and poured everything into that final panting lunge to the finish line. She was truly ready to step out of time into eternity.

Mercy in a Conversation

I was at the foot of Debbie's bed with her immediate family. In the previous few weeks Debbie had become unresponsive, though we had reason to believe that during much of that time she at least was able to hear us talking. We all knew the end was very, very near. But we also knew that in death, even as it had been in life, Debbie's testimony would produce a great harvest.

Jesus said it. "Truly, truly I say to you, unless a grain of wheat falls into the earth and dies, it remains alone, but if it dies, it bears much fruit" (John 12:24). I shared my heart and this verse with my nieces and their parents (Debbie's brother and his wife). It gave me great comfort knowing that Debbie's death was not for nothing, but that instead it would "bear much fruit." That would soon become very clear.

On February 12, I called Joni. She offered some words of hope to Debbie and me that I will never forget:

"It means so much that I have been able to be an encouragement to you. Knowing you'll be with him soon and very soon makes me a little envious of you—just a little. For you heaven is breaking on the horizon. Let me sing for you the song—"I must tell Jesus all of my trials." There's a stanza of a beautiful hymn I love, Debbie. It goes, "Ever lift thy face upon me as I work and wait for thee. Resting 'neath thy smile, Lord Jesus, earth's dark shadows flee. Brightness of the Father's glory, sunshine of my Father's face. Keep me trusting, resting ever, dawn is full of grace." I guess now you are resting 'neath the smile of Jesus.

I just get goose bumps thinking of the weight of glory being accrued on your behalf. Because of your quiet spirit, because of your submissive spirit. You are humbling yourself to the purposes of God and the life of Mark and your life and the life of your church. Thanks for being so obedient, Debbie. It has really inspired me today. I can't tell you how touched I am personally with all this. I wish we weren't a continent apart. You are in my thoughts and prayers, especially over the next few weeks or so."

I replied, "I can see in her eyes how much she appreciates this. Yesterday at church as we closed our time we sang one of Debbie's many, many favorite songs. The songs on your first album speak so much to Debbie's life. Especially the song, 'Though I spend my earthly lifetime in this chair I refuse to waste it living in despair . . .'"

Joni cried over the phone lines as she sang that song for my beloved Beeba. Then she said, "I was thinking of how to pray for you, and I am thinking about those kinds of passages and transitions and how we have one foot in heaven but we really have another foot on earth. We know the reality of death, and it is so true to us. I was re-reading some of your correspondence, and in one of your notes you talked about how expressive Debbie's face had been and about her eyes. I thought that was so poignant, so special. I will be talking about you and about Debbie, sharing your testimony a little bit. She worked in a hospital where she worked with patients with MS, didn't she?"

"Yes," I answered her.

"I was going to mention that to the group and I couldn't remember the exact details. Well, I think that Debbie has reminded us that living with suffering down here on earth is a matter of readjusting our expectations. We ask less of this life because we know more is coming in the next."

"That's for sure," I replied. "Your ministry has so inspired us."

Joni then noted, "I remember how she looked outside at her bird feeder, and that is a reminder of how God attends to their needs and to ours."

"We have a lot to be thankful for, Joni," I agreed. "The hardest thing was for me to let Debbie go. But now there is such a peace in my heart. The grace is just flowing, knowing the Lord will continue to open more doors for blessing."

Joni went on, "Another favorite hymn of mine that is appropriate for this is, 'Finish then Thy new creation, Pure and spotless let us be. Let us see Thy great salvation, perfectly restored in Thee. Glory into glory, till we cast our crowns before thee, lost in wonder love and praise."

I replied, as Debbie now seemed so distant, "She's cheering for me but she does not miss me."

Joni assured me, "Love never fails, which means her love is higher, broader, and greater."

Saying "I Love You," One Last Time

Every year Debbie and I had the opportunity to have a special date on Valentine's Day as the youth of our church prepared a special meal for couples. We eagerly anticipated our date, in part because it gave us a chance to be around other couples. Due to the illness and for reasons that are easy to imagine, we did not have the opportunity to enjoy the fellowship with and presence of other couples in the way most people do. One day a year, though, we had our time.

Our eating routine was not the norm. I would feed Debbie before we left, watching my beloved lady savor some dessert with her bobbing tongue. Then we'd arrive at church for the Valentine's Day banquet. As we arrived on the church property, we'd see the white and colored lights hanging down from tree limbs as decorations, with their reflections glimmering in the water of the azure lake and the small, swift stream. That always brought me to a festive and holiday mood, preparing my heart for our time together that evening.

As we made our way indoors, we'd detect the pleasant music that was playing, music designed to bring a smile to our faces. The young college students in the church had been enlisted to serve the food. They began with hors d'oeuvres, smiling faces darting here and there about the room offering delectable treats to willing diners. Later, those same students would perform skits and songs for us, the young and single entertaining the older and married on the subject of romance. Then someone would read a Scripture and offer a few words of encouragement about what God intends for real romance to be. We always left those dates feeling rekindled in our love for each other.

I realized that the others there were reminded by our presence of just how much they had to be thankful for. At the same time I knew they could see the kindled glow of God's love in our relationship, and they seemed to both look up to us and feel sorrow for us. Our life was filled with those kinds of ambiguities. Couples often commented to me that just being around us with our unique situation strengthened their own marriages. Our college-age servers also received from us a sober reminder that one day, one might have to take seriously that vow—for better, for worse.

For me, the promise of "for better or for worse" was a solemn agreement with a binding force. The choice I made to keep my precious Beeba in "our palace" was not dependent on her behavior but on that promise. Over time I came to know that God's promises are unbroken and unending. Learning how God takes his promises seriously and seals them with his own oath inspired me to keep my own vow. I knew those college-age students did not know all of that as they stood and nervously glanced at us during our Valentine's dates, but perhaps they got some hint of it. I hope they did. In any case, those were special days for my Beeba and for me.

This year would be different. I began to see her food building up in the refrigerator—though we still tried to feed her, she could not swallow it at all anymore. A deep pit welled up in my heart. My precious wife was weaker than I'd ever imagined. The imminent specter of death was staring us in the face. I knew we could not go out for our annual date, but that did not mean that I was not going to express my passion for the wife of my dreams for this one last romantic holiday. I bought a Valentine's cookie, hoping against hope that she would be able to enjoy the sweetness in her mouth. I wanted it to remind her of all of the sweet times we'd had together on other Valentine's Day celebrations. Only a couple of very small bites melted in her mouth, however. There was virtually no response—only a slight blink of her eyes.

She seemed more distant from me now than ever she had, and yet, at the same time, somehow even closer. My heart was breaking inside my chest as I knew this would be the last Valentine's Day I would ever celebrate with my beloved wife, and this time we'd be alone as others enjoyed the customary ambiance. That vessel of precious clay was now deteriorated to the shattering point. There was no way to reverse that. I knew eternity for Debbie was close, but what I did not know was that we would have only two more days together as husband and wife in this world.

The Hour of Departure

February 16, 1996, began with light snow. I had a problem at work and needed to go in to straighten things out, even though I wanted to stay at home with my rapidly deteriorating wife. To be frank, however, I must admit work had become something of a temporary escape for me in those dark days—the issues at work were fixable. I suppose it was somewhat therapeutic for me to be the "fix-it" guy where that was possible. My mother and father were at the house with Becky, who had returned from South Carolina to her nursing post at her best friend's deathbed.

A couple of hours later Becky called me at the office. "I really think you need to come home to be with Debbie right now." It had been snowing more than I realized. About six inches of snow covered the ground, and the iciness of the road was matched by the chill I felt in my own heart as I started my car and pulled out on the street. I pulled up to the major intersection outside my office only to find that the traffic was gridlocked.

I turned on my speaker-phone as I hurriedly called and spoke to Becky. I asked her to put the speaker on at the house as well so the Debbie could hear my voice. I began to pray aloud on the phone and encouraged and coached my wife as well as I could. Periodically breaking into tears, I was singing hymns on the phone and praying out loud all the way home. I forced the car through the snowdrifts and pulled up to the house. I leapt out of the car and rushed inside. Becky was urging me over and over, "Please hurry, Mark." I rushed into the house with boots full of snow. I went right into the bedroom with my jacket and boots still on, hoping against hope I was not too late. Her face, under the oxygen mask assisting her labored breathing, was so dusky and drawn.

For years her body had been moving ever more surely into a sort of fetal position. It had been a long time since I could hold her normally, and that in itself had been heartbreaking, since holding your wife face-to-face is such an important part of the marital bond. Now her knees had drawn up even further towards her chest. Restraining myself from bursting into a wail, I climbed into bed with her and hugged her tightly from behind.

I began to pray and sing in her ear. I was weeping and yet my prayer and the words of my mouth were rejoicing words. "You are almost there." I was trying to tell her one more time of my love for her. "You have been the love and center of my life. You have led me in so many ways to a transformation of my character."

My mother was crying as she watched her firstborn son in his anguish. I could feel my wife's body stiffening and relaxing—struggling, I believe, to say something to me in those final seconds of life on this side of eternity. This went on for five minutes, ten minutes, a little longer. Who knows? Time was a blur.

Here was my young wife, only thirty-eight years old, and her broken and emaciated body was losing its struggle, a battle she fought for almost half of her entire earthly sojourn. Here was a moment we knew would come. But all the preparation could not have readied us completely for this moment that was awful yet glorious at the same time. Facing death is never easy, and it always carries with it the recognition that there is a great enemy of the human race out there. It always brings grief, but not a hopeless grief for believers. And since we suspected for some time that Debbie's illness would one day kill her, we were both ready for it and also rejoicing in the glory of her home-going.

It was one of those events in which time itself seemed to stand stock-still. The minutes were so filled with significance that every second seemed to stretch out endlessly. She struggled, stiffened, and wrestled as much as her weakened and petite body could. Yet, it was probably less than twenty minutes after I arrived at the house that she would slip away from us.

It was as if she answered to a voice speaking to her heart, a voice that may have said, "It is time. Come to me. The best is about to begin." She stopped struggling. And she was gone. It was then so absolutely clear to me that her spirit had fled. She was gone, and all that remained was the broken shell, the shattered clay of a life lived gloriously before the Master Potter.

As I held her, it was evident that the core of her being had somehow departed. She was the one my heart beat in tandem with, my life long 'helpmeet' and companion, the "wind beneath my wings," and now she was gone. This woman had been my prayer warrior, my lovely wife with the unforgettable smile, always cheering me on. She was my encourager in the battle, the one I lived to love, the one I had loved to provide for. Her life was a message of faith far more profound than any message I could ever speak to a group of people.

Several weeks earlier I had spoken at our church service. Debbie was there with me, unmoving in her wheelchair, face immobile and no longer able to show emotion. I spoke of the fact that I knew that Debbie was about to be taken from me. It was heart-wrenching, yet I told the people listening that I knew it was the will of God. Then I knelt before my wife in her wheelchair, and sang to her Joni's song, "Heaven Is Nearer to Me."

I don't know how much Debbie was able to sort out just what was happening in that moment, since the final stages of the illness were already raging in her body, but I know she understood the truth of what I was singing. She had known that truth for a long time, and she understood it far better than I did.

I got up from Debbie's death bed with a bit of a smile on my face. Tears flowing, I started to praise God. I am not usually a highly demonstrative or emotional worshipper in the way many of our more "charismatic" brothers and sisters are, but you might have disagreed with that statement if you had seen me! I was thrilled to know her battle finally was over. But I was at the same time grieving and rejoicing, oscillating between weeping and praising God.

I can't help but think this is the way it ought to be—a sad sweetness. It was a bitter joy that I knew in my heart at that moment, and it seemed this was exactly the way it should have been. The thought came to me that especially in those last days, and even more so in those final minutes, Debbie and I were so very close, as if we were one person. And yet we were not. She would now ultimately stand alone—before God himself—awaiting the final phase of her redemption.

Chapter 14

In the Master Potter's Hands

Facing a New Reality

NOW I WAS set adrift like an iceberg broken away from a glacier and making its way slowly to a new destination. For the first time since the beginning of her illness I felt truly alone. All of my life had centered on her, and now she had left me behind and was before the presence of God. The separation that occurs at death is profound. In a sense this was an extremely quiet moment, with only quiet weeping from some in the room. But it was a silence that was almost deafening.

Eric Hoffer once wrote, "It is loneliness that makes the loudest noise." I know exactly what that means. But this was not loneliness based on self-pity. I did not feel sorry for myself. There was no point in that. When you know the Lord, you don't have to feel self-pity. Rather, you can focus on what you have, not on what you have lost. In my case, I could focus both on what I now had as well as what I had been given in those wonderful years of marriage. Debbie's death had not taken that from me. Our story was no tragedy such as that of Romeo and Juliet, or some other tale of doomed lovers. No, ours was the story of a great victory of the gift of faith over despair. It was the triumph of love against great obstacles and of Christ over the forces of evil. When Debbie slipped quietly into eternity, the Devil lost. Christ had won! Now she was fully made new, a vessel of eternal, incorruptible, shatterproof beauty.

A good friend stopped by. I appreciated his desire to show his respect and concern, but I needed space. He was gracious and did not stay long. I needed to have some time to myself to sort out my own feelings. I needed some moments for closure. Even though I had prepared myself, or I thought I had, I discovered that no one is ever really prepared for such a moment. Feelings flooded my mind I had not expected. It reminded me that it is impossible to be completely prepared for the unknown.

You think you are ready for anything, especially when you have thought through the process over and over again through the course of many years. You think you know how you will react when confronted by the moment when it finally arrives. You may even rehearse your response over and over again. But if you presume you will always be able to respond in the right way, you are probably fooling yourself. It is never exactly like you expect.

Your mouth gets dry, and a thousand different scenarios run through your head. Your chest tightens. You feel alone. It's not what you thought it would be. This is just another reason why you really need the Lord in such moments. Your own resources are just not enough, not even the ones you have been preparing for years. If anyone feels completely sufficient to face such moments in isolation, then that person truly does not understand.

I finally called the mortician, a small, reserved man. It was obvious he had done this duty more than a few times. That snowy day he did a simple, quiet deed for someone in need, like giving a cup of water to someone in the name of the Lord. I was grateful. When he and an assistant arrived, I did not want to leave the room. Just letting them take her seemed like such an act of finality. My Beeba would finally be gone, but I just did not want some anonymous person who "does this for a living" taking care of these final duties without my being involved in whatever way I could. This was the lady I loved and cared for and cooked for and dressed and laughed with. I wanted to see her out the door one last time.

They put her body in a body bag. The process seemed so unceremonious—a body bag like the ones they put criminals in, or anonymous people who die in an accident. Surely my beloved deserved something better than a simple body bag! It was just procedure, of course, but it just seemed so low, so disrespectful. This was a great woman, and she was just being zipped up in a piece of plastic and carried out of my house. Did she not deserve better? I realize now that such thoughts are not very logical, but I was not very rational at the moment. I suppose no one ever is.

I began to flash back to the image of my dream girl. I was thinking about the time we met, when we fell in love. Then I thought of the first carriage house, and how happy it made her. I thought of carrying her across our threshold as we returned from our honeymoon. Then the dream house we built, and how it had served us so well in the years of her illness. I thought of Debbie's glowing face and her big smile and how she loved listening to Joni's radio program and her music. I remembered our ministry to the disabled and what joy that brought to my wife.

I thought of Becky and how she changed our lives so much for the better by her friendship and by her loving care for and treatment of my wife. I remembered the trip to the West, which turned out being our great final journey together. Then those last few months of rapid decline and deadly deterioration. Now Debbie was being removed in a black plastic body bag. Though I had carried her back and forth from chair to bed to car for years, I could not carry her to her final destination.

The undertaker stood solemnly by the door and looked at me. He said simply, "My wife died. I am remarried. It will never be the same." It was as if his words simply fell dead on the floor. But this unhappy comment, this quiet deed, attached to a sad and dreary moment, in some odd way deeply ministered to me.

Light from the Shattered Jar

I understand that United States presidents are asked to make preparations for their funerals right after coming to office. After all, when you are a president, you never know when death may come. Pope Julius the Warrior began constructing his tomb immediately after becoming pope, and he and Michelangelo had many arguments about that over the years.

I imagine most people don't think much about their own funeral until they start aging, or maybe until discovering a potentially terminal illness. Over the years I thought a great deal about Debbie's funeral. I wanted her home-going celebration to be joyful and triumphant. I wanted it to be a celebration, but I did not want levity. I knew it could go either way, considering the kinds of emotions that Debbie stirred up in people over the years. I knew I wanted to provide a God-honoring and serious environment for her memorial.

Debbie's mom and dad stayed at my house the night before her home-going funeral celebration. My father-in-law made a profession of faith in my study the night before the funeral. It was one more example of what I have already addressed—that when the grain of wheat dies it bears much fruit. The home-going service was packed with people. I spoke, and so did some close friends. Then the next morning as her little body, now housed in a sealed casket, was lowered into the ground the gratitude that overwhelmed me broke forth in my words. Nonetheless the reality was striking. Ashes to ashes, dust to dust. Clay is corruptible—it disintegrates and reverts to the ground.

People from our church, from our disability ministry, medical people who had known and worked with Debbie—all kinds of people attended her home-going celebration. We sang her favorite hymns and songs. I shared from my heart that the Lord gives and the Lord takes away. Blessed be the name of the Lord! I wept and I laughed. Even as I had done before a crowd of witnesses years before, I once again publicly professed my love for my dear wife. She was more beautiful to me now as I lay her to rest than she was nearly two decades earlier when she became my wife. In front of those gathered, I thanked God for my precious Beeba, my jar of broken, shattered, yet now restored and eternally beautiful clay.

Living in this world broken and twisted by sin, Debbie's death stood as mute testimony to what God can do in a person's life. Though her little broken form lay lifeless in a casket, yet from her had streamed forth life. Though her world was darkened by her inability to see and respond, her heart was filled with the kind of light which, many ages ago, first ignited the sun and stars and brought its beauty to a place where "darkness covered the face of the deep" (Genesis 1:2). Debbie's body ultimately succumbed to the reality of death, but her spirit never did.

As much as I loved her on earth, my love for her will be made complete in the heavenly realm. I know Jesus said there is no marriage or giving of marriage in heaven, but I believe relationships we had in this life will still be precious to us in the life to come. Remember that after his resurrection, Jesus had great affection for those he knew in his earthly sojourn. I am eagerly anticipating seeing Debbie again as she once was—whole and healthy and filled with energy. In fact, she will be greater than I have ever known her since she will be imperishable, powerful, spiritual, and glorious (1 Corinthians 15:42–44). I know that now Debbie has no limitations on her life and health. I rejoice in that for her, and I just look forward to rejoicing with her in that freedom in heaven.

One day I will join Debbie in eternal glory. I also know that my love for her in this life, while it was often wonderful, was never complete, never a perfect love. I often felt the pang of guilt for the fact that I knew my love always fell short of the ideal. My own self and my own needs so often interfered with my ability to love my wife with complete selfishness. This was a constant struggle for me, though few people watching from the outside would have guessed it. But one day I will be finally transformed so that I will no longer bear in my body the limitations and baggage that sin brings with it. At that time I will love her fully and completely. I will love her with a love that knows no selfishness and no limitations. I will love her with the true *agape* (completely *selfless*) love that comes only from the Father, who is himself love.

There is more. God loves our bodies. He made them in the first place, and this means he is not merely interested in our souls, but in ourselves as whole persons. This is one of the reasons that sin is such a terrible thing. It ravages the goodness God originally created in the material world. This world contained animals and trees, oceans and stars. All of it was affected by sin, but the most tragic result was what happened to humans, God's highest creation. Because of sin they become frail, ill, and they die.

If salvation in the final stages means a reversal of all that, then it means all infirmities of life will eventually be cast away. We get heaven when we die, but the final hope is the resurrection of the dead in glorified bodies that will never again have even the possibility of frailty, decay, or death. It is eternal life in physical bodies, but bodies that have been transformed into something that will never again know weakness or infirmity. At the time of the second coming of Christ, my Debbie and all of those who have died as believers in Jesus will be raised with imperishable bodies, and in that state they will "always be with the Lord" (1 Thessalonians 4:17).

What a beautiful thought! If you have ever faced the ravages of sickness or the infirmity that comes with advancing age, you know exactly what I mean. There is nothing more encouraging than to know that one day we will have the final say over the enemies of this age. Sin, death and the Devil will one day be defeated forever. We will watch as they are cast into the lake of fire. The twentieth chapter of the book of Revelation promises us we will never again have to face opponents of their like again.

Amen! Come, Lord Jesus!

Time to Think

Once the funeral was over, I took a lot of time thinking about things. I wondered what the things were that sustained Debbie and me during all those years of the struggle. Prayer, Christian fellowship, God's Word and promises, Debbie's mother, and Debbie herself came to mind.

So many people prayed for us. Many people prayed for us we did not even know, people we never met. Sometimes I think we feel that prayers are just perfunctory. "Well, that is just something Christian people do." Maybe that is true with some. It may be just a formality in the experience of many. But if you go through the kind of ordeal we endured, your prayers will no longer just be a formality. Prayer becomes real because in prayer God becomes more and more real in a personal and experiential way. Face genuine trauma, and you will have the sense in prayer that you really are talking to the God of the universe, and you will also know he is listening.

Fellowship was another important thing in our ability to be overcomers. God becomes real when he is real in the lives of others who want to bless us. Fellowship with God generally includes fellowship with others. When you encounter genuine Christians who want to minister to you it is like meeting God with skin on him. That is something we all need—God with skin on him. Please understand, I don't really mean that they are God, but that they come in his name to make a difference in our lives.

People sometimes came along the way and asked how we were doing. Others avoided the topic, as if they were fearful they might embarrass one or the other of us. Suffering people do not want to avoid the topic, nor do they simply want lots of sympathy. People whose suffering is obvious to all know they are the objects of attention wherever they go. They don't want to be stared at, and yet they don't want to be nervously ignored. They want to find a way to achieve some kind of normalcy with those around them. They also want to find a way to serve and they want others to find a way to serve, as well. Often people seem to pray, "God use me." Since we know that God wants to use us, maybe a better prayer would be, "Lord, make me usable."

On the other hand, there were key people along the way I expected support from but did not get. By choosing not to engage, they have no idea what they missed. Debbie had some friends who stopped being her friends when she became seriously ill. Some people cannot cope with tragedy and cannot stay committed to those living with pain and suffering. It may be that in some cases they just can't face the thought that some day they may endure something similar. It may be that they only want beautiful things in their lives. Of course, when you walk the path of pain, you change your mind about what genuine beauty actually is. I know. It happened to me in just that way.

Debbie's mother Florence and I had wonderful times in loving my wife and her daughter. I will always be grateful to her for that. You always expect that loved ones will step up to the plate and be responsible when you need them. But when they go above and beyond the call of duty, as Florence did, it always makes you so grateful for what God has placed in your path.

And finally, Debbie herself sustained me during all those years of the struggle. During those years, she never complained. I was not as sensitive as I should have been much of the time, especially in the early years, even after Christ drew us to himself. Yet, she was so willing to give me space when I needed it.

We made it! Yes, in 1996 my lovely Beeba succumbed to the ravages of the illness and breathed her last breath in the seen world. But we made it anyway. We won—or rather, Christ won. We fought the good fight of faith and endured the race set before us. The Enemy did not beat us. By the grace of God and with the help of many others who ran the race with us, we became overcomers, and we will meet again in the unseen world.

The home-coming was over. Then reality hit. I had given most of my adult life to serving both Debbie and God, with Debbie alongside me, the woman of my dreams who was given to me by God. Now, on the precipice of age forty, I wondered—what was the next part of God's plan?

"All the days ordained for me are written in your book before one of them came to be" Psalm 139:16.

Debbie With Her Brother Glenn

Debbie's Early Twirling Days

188

A Portrait Of Beauty

Beginnings Of Mark And Debbie

Courtship In Love

Our Wedding Day

Our First Dream Home

Over The Threshold

My life was just like China, a lovely thing to me but fragile things do slip and fall.

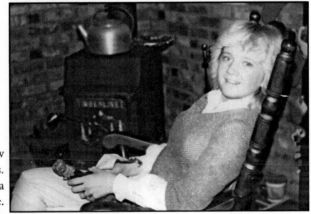

The diagnosis—a new season is upon us. Now learning to live a dying life.

When Pretty Things Get Broken

A Window God's Light Shown Through

Debbie With "Mandy"

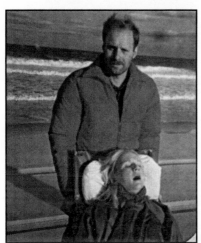

Trip To The Shore

Mark With His Dad

Mark Begins
Building Their
New Dream
Home

The Pleasure Of
Showing My Bride
Around

If only you could
really see!

Another Anniversary
Camping Trip

Believer's Baptism

The Best Seat In The Chapel

A Serenade From Bob

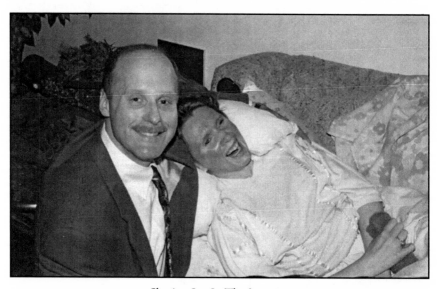

Sharing Joy In The Journey

Fun In The Sun

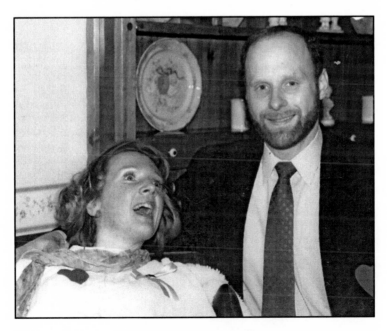

Valentines Day—Favorite Times

Disability Ministry

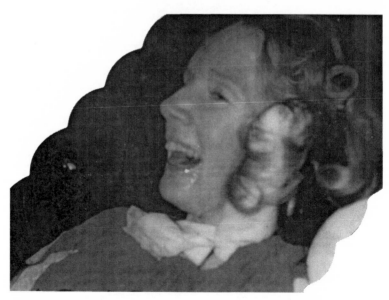

Who Cares About Drooling? "I'm Havin' Fun."

A Horse Drawn Sleigh

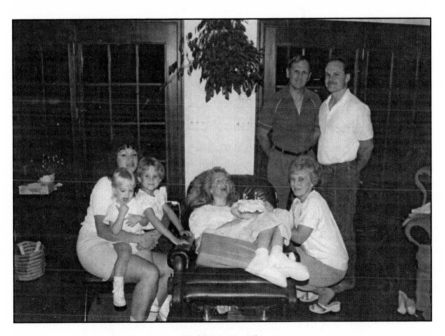

Debbie's Family

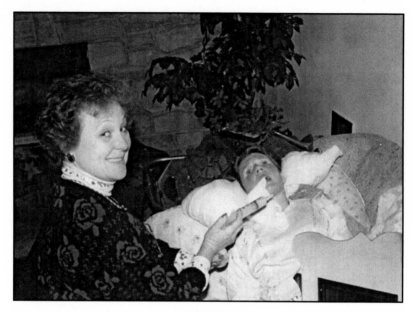

Mark's Mom

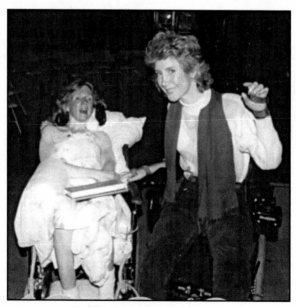

Debbie Meets Her Faith Hero

A Special Sister And Friend

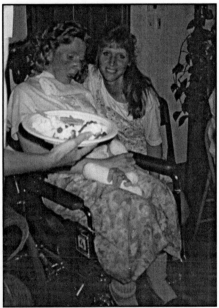

Surprise Birthday Party

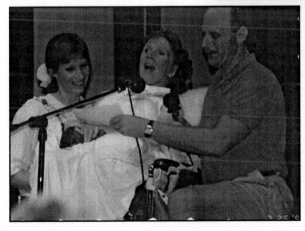

Singing Together At JAF
Ministries Retreat

"Another Window God's Light Shown Through"

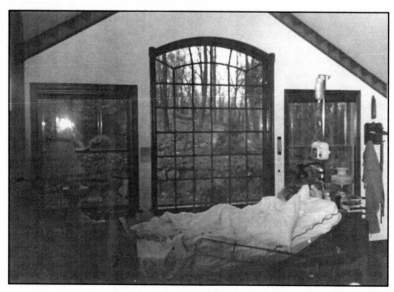

Time To Pray

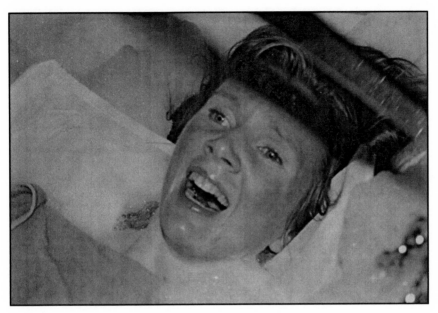

Ahh . . . Whirlpool Bath

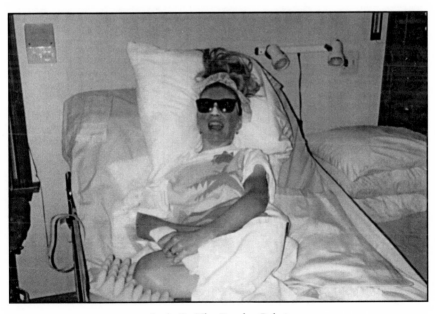

Let's Go The Beach - Babe!

As I spend my mortal lifetime in this chair I refuse to waste it living in despair.

Sharing Laughs

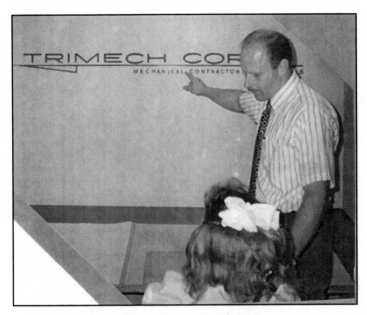

Mark Brings Debbie To TRIMECH

Debbie Desperately Trying To Appreciate The Visit

Heading Out
Cross Country
Love Poured Out

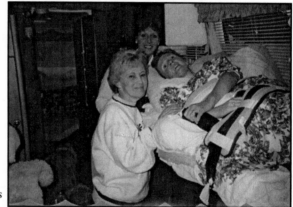

Her Best Of Friends

Whispering Sweet
Nothings

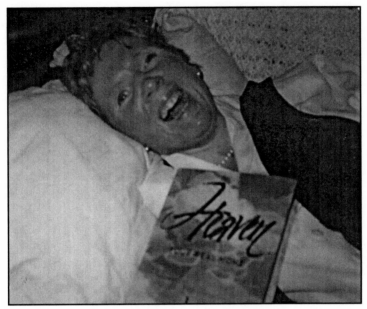

Longing For Heaven—My Real Home

The Final Lap Of The Race

Goodbye For Now My Love

My Favorite Smile

Newly Molded from Shattered Pieces

~❦~

Welcome Rest for the Battle Weary

CONFEDERATE SOLDIERS WHO signed up to fight in the early days of the Civil War in 1861 thought they were enlisting only for a few months, or a year at most. The majority of them only agreed to a one-year long commitment. The war, however, lasted for four years, and no one was allowed out of the army except those who had been so badly wounded that they could no longer serve. That was four long, exhausting years of warfare; I had just completed almost seventeen years of a very different kind of fight.

With the funeral behind me, a sort of anti-climax settled in. I was weary and suffering from the effects of loss. Healing is a process that can take a long, long time, and even to this day I periodically have a painfully vivid dream where I meet Debbie alive on this earth, still suffering and under someone else's inadequate care. As if I had abandoned her, I awake, believing the dream to be true. I am always guilt ridden in the dream, finding myself filled with relief when I awake and realize it was only a dream. Both my mind and body felt the impact of the trial then, and I still do today. I guess I am still dealing with the fog that some times lingers in the air for awhile even after the rain has stopped falling. I needed a way to clear my head and to get perspective on the steps that lay before me. As the song says, "I can see clearly now, the rain is gone." That clarity of vision was what I was looking for.

After the home-going service, I had to get away. I decided to take a trip to see my sister in Buffalo, New York. I had not been able to take a drive like that alone for many years. Now I was on the road, and as the mile markers clicked by I was able to reflect on and evaluate just where I was in my own personal journey, a journey that was merging onto a new path.

Like a symbol of my life thus far, one stretch of highway closed behind me as another opened before me. What was behind was familiar, thousands of distinct moments I replayed over and over again through the years as we sought to understand and cope with the challenges of our life together. All those moments were still there, though the perception of my experience with them would slowly change in the days ahead. What was not entirely clear was what lay before me. I had some ideas of what would happen, but when you are on a road you have never traveled before, you can't be entirely sure what is over the next hill, nor can you know for certain how you will react to what you encounter along the way.

One thing I know, I wept for Debbie over the next few days, sometimes uncontrollably, more than I had wept up to that time. I could not believe she was gone. The reality of her pain and suffering had become so much a part of our existence that it seemed unthinkable she had been freed from it. While Debbie was living, I did not want her to be taken away from me, but at the same time I longed for her to be free from the pain and suffering she was enduring and in the arms of the Bridegroom of the church. Now that she was gone, I struggled with many of the same emotions, wanting her back, but knowing how much better her life now was.

My sister welcomed me into her home and family. It had been a long time since we had been able to spend time together just as brother and sister. Debbie and I had had the kind of issues that caused us to be almost totally consumed with our own internal family concerns, and there had been little time or energy for the wider family. With some key exceptions, we lived almost in isolation from our families. It was refreshing to be able to spend time, at ease and at peace, with my sister and her family and not to have Debbie on my mind the whole time, wondering if she were being cared for and if she needed me. She was now beyond my help and in the hands of the Great Physician. Never again would she need a doctor or a nurse or a hovering husband to provide for her daily needs and comforts.

Often in those days I thought about her in her heavenly body, completely free from pain and suffering, knowing that her beautiful face was now creased with the most glowing smile possible. I wept in the first few days out of a sense of my own loss and emptiness that my Precious Beeba had been taken from me. At the end of my visit with family, my tears were turning into tears of joy that Debbie was whole again, more whole than she had ever been. The future is always more important than the past. That is a lesson we have to learn and re-learn, and one we must apply to our lives in many different ways.

Death and Resurrection–of a Church

We knew Debbie would be raised in a glorious resurrection. In spite of that confidence, during Debbie's last days the smell of death was in the air in more ways than one. My business partner's moral failings and bad decisions had led to an ongoing crisis at my company—in fact, the one that had been occupying my attention early in the morning the day Debbie passed away. While I did have hope that my company's issues would eventually be resolved, I wasn't so hopeful about our church's future.

I was serving on the elder board until just before Debbie's final downturn. Suddenly we were faced with the reality that we as a church had a major problem, a full-blown situation that seemed to spell the congregation's doom. It had a history stretching back over a year before Debbie's death. People had given all their efforts and much money to their beloved church only to find themselves betrayed by an authority figure. The congregation's security was threatened. People can forgive many things of a spiritual leader, but understandably they have a very difficult time coping when they feel their trust has been so blatantly betrayed.

While there was usually strong biblical teaching and a wonderful commitment on the part of the people in the congregation, it was becoming more and more clear that financial mismanagement had also occurred, that the discipleship model our church taught was flawed, and that some of the other teachings were skewed. There were also aspects of control that clearly crossed the line of healthy church dynamics. The line between truth and error is sometimes a subtle one, and sometimes even the truth can be mismanaged. Heresies and even milder false teachings often have some form of the truth, but a form of the truth that ignores aspects of the whole truth. These can often be promoted and propagated in some terrible and destructive ways.

Most of the details are not germane to my story here. Suffice it to say, though, that we have to recognize that the church is a body and it only has one head, and that head is not the pastor or elders, important as these shepherds and overseers are. There were meetings and there were hurt feelings. Most people in the church felt our situation required that something dramatic be done.

Meanwhile, some people in the community who objected to the autocratic leadership structure in the church were even accusing it of being a cult. It just seemed we were going from the frying pan into the fire. And in my own life, more than one fire was burning at the same time. Where and when would it all end?

Many of my good brothers and sisters in the Lord believed it was God's will that our church fail. This was an extremely hard thing to face. I read teaching in the Bible that "the gates of Hades" would not prevail against the church (Matthew 16:18). I knew this meant Christ would triumph and that his church would remain strong no matter what. But of course that refers to the church universal and does not mean local congregations will not fail. Individual congregations *have* gone out of existence—thousands of them since the days of the early church.

We decided to follow a strategy to allow the church to die in the form in which it had existed. We stopped services. We did not encourage our members to continue to fight for survival. People mostly left. We essentially said to them, "We are going to have a new start, but feel free to make a new life somewhere else if you feel that is the right thing for you." Only twenty to thirty people decided to stay.

The remaining members continued to meet, but primarily to study the Bible and pray together. We went for many months with no pastor. We wanted the kind of healing that can only come with time. Like a jilted lover, we felt our one hope to recover in the long run was to get space and time between our former existence as a church and any future such existence we might have as a congregation. All of this was happening during the months that my beloved faded increasingly into death's repose. God never promised that life would be simple. I learned that lesson over and over again in the years 1995 and 1996.

After we went a sufficient amount of time without actually functioning as a church, we then re-organized into another church. As late as November, 1997, over two years after the crisis within the church had erupted, our survival as an identifiable local congregation was still in question. But we persisted, and we kept meeting. I had been serving as the elder board's spokesman through this difficult process. We encouraged one another. We rediscovered the plethora of gifts and ministries already present in our fellowship. Somehow God just gave us a new sense of hope and confidence as the year 1998 marched along.

We officially reconstituted on June 1, 1998. On September 16 of that year we affirmed our affiliation a wonderful evangelical association of churches preaching the gospel and affirming the Scriptures as the true Word of God. On November 15, 1998, we celebrated the birth of our new church. It was a great day. I knew that my Beeba was alive in heaven with the Lord, and now our fellowship had experienced a kind of resurrection of its own.

Sensing the Molding of the Potter's Hands

At this point let me backtrack a little to recount the personal aspects of the first weeks and months without Debbie. After I returned from my trip to see my sister, I began to consider what God's plan was for my future. Debbie was my one-and-only, my *soul mate*. The ancient Greek playwright Aristophanes coined the term soul mate. He believed that in the original creation people were made both male and female at the same time, with two heads, two sets of arms and legs and so on. In that condition, they were in complete harmony and happiness. But Zeus, the king of the gods, hated the blissfulness of mankind and hurled a thunderbolt, separating the genders. Now, according to Aristophanes, one's only hope for happiness is to find that person they were separated from—literally, one's *soul mate.*

That is a silly myth, of course, but in Debbie I believed I found the one person meant for me. She really was the perfect mate, and I think she thought the same of me. It was as if God gave me the one woman I would love with the kind of passion I knew little about on the day of our wedding. But in the crucible of life, the Lord gifted me with that passion, so that I sought to love her as Christ loves the church.

Now Debbie was gone. And if she was the one woman for me, what was I to think about the possibility of finding another woman? Might it be that God in his mercy would give me another wife? It seemed that he was willing to do that.

Was that right? In the second century a group of Christians known as the Montanists said it was a sin for widows or widowers to remarry. They said it was a sin for two reasons. First, it was wrong because a person would only want to remarry so that he might have conjugal relations. The Montanists believed that sex, even between married people, was a sin. Second, they argued that if one's spouse died one must have not taken very good care of that spouse, and therefore, God would not provide another one.

Well, I can't imagine that any Christians today would accept the notion that sex within marriage is wrong. And in my case, it would have been unlikely for someone to allege I had not been a good steward of my wife or of our relationship together. But what about marrying again? Could someone else also be my soul mate, or just a replacement of the wife who was now gone?

There was also the question of *when* I might remarry. Is there a period of time that would be considered good form? How long would that period of waiting be? Six months? A year? Two years? How would I know?

Within only a short time after Debbie's funeral, Becky and I both became convinced God was bringing us together. We had worked together closely within one of the most intense kind of environments ever imaginable, and our knowledge of each other's strengths and weaknesses went back not months but years. I'd seen her in her bad moments and she certainly saw me in mine.

When people work closely in a crisis situation, one which exacts the most extreme kinds of emotions, it is not unusual for a bond to form. Becky and I sought God's grace in keeping that bond in its context all of that time—the context of people working together and forming a close friendship. In a way we were like employees of the same company working together, but whose eyes are always on the task and not on each other.

But now that bond began quickly to develop into one between a man and a woman. That is a very different kind of bond. It just seemed natural that our relationship would transform into something other than what it had been.

Of course, there was a mutual affection. We had also had a deep respect for each other. There was also physical attraction—Becky is a beautiful woman. There was also spiritual and moral regard for one another. This may be the most important component of all, since to love someone means that you have respect for that person's moral character. These are all components necessary to a good marriage. But they are really not enough simply left to themselves.

Sometimes Christian authors make romantic love and the question of marriage too complicated. At the base of it, for me, there are two simple questions: Does she love Jesus? Am I crazy about her? There might be more to it if the lovers in question are eighteen years old, but we were not eighteen years old. I knew that Becky loved Jesus and as the weeks went by I began to realize I was falling in love with her. I was also becoming confident that she was perfect for me and I was perfect for her, at least as perfect as one can be in a world made of human beings fallen in sin. It was as if God had given to me a second person who was right for me in every way. I was beginning to feel blessed in a new and refreshing way.

I shared with Becky that Debbie had given us her blessing in the final days of her life. Often we would both break down as we realized how powerfully God had been at work though this process as he had kept our focus in those days on her. He somehow ensured the fact that our feelings would not be a potential barrier to my ministry to Debbie in her declining days. We reflected on the wisdom provided for us as he opened the door for Becky to go to her parents' home, then to work at some other nursing jobs in the waning months of 1995. That break was a good thing in many ways for both of us. But now those things had changed. If God really brought us together, and we believed he had, when should we make that known to family and friends? And when should we act on our conviction?

Ends and Beginnings

I invited Becky to dinner. It was more than just a time for us to talk about what we had just been through, although it was that, too. We met at the Chateau Hathorne, a Swiss restaurant that is one of my favorite places. Because it was a quiet week night, there were only a few others in the whole restaurant. She drove herself there and we met and hugged each other like old friends who have shared a deep and profound experience. And yet, there was clearly something more to that hug than just the embrace of friends. We had been companions in a common cause, co-workers with an urgent task to perform. But that God-ordained mission was now complete, and any relationship we would have in the future would have to stand on a different set of legs.

It seemed it was more appropriate for us to drive to our meeting separately, rather than to drive there together. We were not quite ready to get into a car together and to drive off somewhere like people in the state of courtship. And, anyway, was it courtship? I didn't know. I hoped it could be. I did know we needed some time to sort things out, time to exhale very deeply before we could inhale new air. We were on the boundary of what our relationship had been during the past years, and the days ahead would determine whether we were going to enlarge those boundaries. Time would tell, and perhaps even this dinner together might give us a clue.

Becky looked absolutely beautiful as she walked in the door of the restaurant. She seemed to allow a reserved glow as she looked at me. In my view this was a welcome statement, to say the least. It seemed surreal. She was very attractive, but now I could look at her differently. I was very excited at seeing her, for more than one reason. I was looking at the woman who was the most important helper in caring for my wife in her last years of life.

Becky's care for Debbie had meant the world to me. For hours and hours on end, day after day, this young woman ministered selflessly to the love of my life. Much beyond the call of duty of even a nurse and friend, she poured her life into Debbie. She read to her, prayed with her, sang to her, talked to her. Often she would even massage her feet and neck and then would doll her up for her husband's return. In the quiet hours of the day when no one else was around, Becky had given her very life to my wife, and had done it with joy in her heart, never grudgingly, never reluctantly, never asking what was in it for her.

Becky loved Debbie, and that love meant more to Debbie than anyone will ever know. This met a special need in Debbie's heart that no husband could have provided. In the book of Samuel in the Old Testament the Lord enabled the Israelites to defeat one of their worst enemies, the Philistines. In the aftermath of the battle the prophet Samuel set up a large stone as a memorial, and named it "Ebenezer," which means "stone of help" (1 Samuel 7). This is what Becky was to me—my stone of help. She stood strong for both Debbie and me when the days were dark and the struggle was intense. She was my Ebenezer, my rock of help, over and over again.

In that restaurant, I was looking at the woman who had been such an invaluable aid to me, simplifying my life at a time when it had been more complex than ever. Even more importantly, because I knew Debbie was in such good hands, Becky helped mitigate the relentless emotional pain I endured watching my wife suffer daily. .But I was also seeing a woman I believed was now going to play an even greater role in my future than in my past.

We shed some quiet tears and we smiled a lot. We were both thinking through not just what lay behind us but also what lay before us. What did our future hold? Was God preparing us for a life together, one that would grow out of what we had shared in the past? How can you find the answer to such questions? What was very clear was that God was completely in control of this heavenly course of events.

When Debbie and I were planning to marry, I believed that when you know, *you just know*. I still believe that. In that simple meeting with

Becky, though my mind was awhirl with emotions and thoughts, I knew God brought us together and that this was not to be the end of it. It was a whole new day. I knew that God had prepared us for each other, both in the distant past and in our recent experiences together.

After a wonderful dinner I began to approach the conversation more carefully. I wanted to say some things to her I could never have said before, and I was feeling my way around to communicate now. What to say and how to say it—that was my challenge, so fresh was the hour of difficulty that lay just behind us.

I was not a newcomer to romance. I had had several girlfriends before Debbie and I married. But Becky was twelve years younger than this "old guy." Besides being younger and thus less "experienced" than me, I recalled that she had once been perplexed about her future with a young man she had dated. I had even counseled her near the end of that relationship by assuring her that "when you know . . . you really know."

I told Becky that I knew God brought her to us when I most needed someone to help me with my wife. She truly was my "stone of help." But now I knew God had brought her to me for more than helping with Debbie. Now that Debbie had gone to be with the Lord, I believed Becky was sent to me by God for a second reason—to be my wife. And what is more appropriate than that one who has been your friend might also become your wife?

I began to feel somewhat awkward, as if I had never before been in the presence of a female. I told her, "I feel like the kid who has borrowed his father's Buick and is on his first date." Moments later I looked at her romantically. I kissed her. This was the first time this dear maiden had ever kissed a guy. What a gift. She had safeguarded her vessel of precious clay for this moment. How blessed could I be!

We talked some more about our future together, and then Becky drove away in her own car. I was filled with a sense of wonder at what God might have in store for us in the days ahead. I pulled out of the restaurant parking lot, wrestling with more emotions than I could ever hope to unpack, even if I had a lifetime to do it.

The Potter Molds Two Into One

So now "we knew." We knew, but we didn't know when the time would be best. Being the romantic that I am, one Saturday summer morning I asked her if she would like to spend the day hiking. I deceived her, in order to surprise her, by telling her that I wanted her to meet my friend and spiritual mentor Oleh.

I greeted her with a bouquet of white roses. She was so excited that she wanted to carry them on the hike with us! I tried to convince her to put them aside in water but she carried them with her all day long. The outdoor flowers were also in bloom and the air was crisp.

I asked her the question that would make it official in a romantic mountain-top gazebo. But just before I did, I discretely asked a nearby couple to take our picture, explaining that I was about to propose to her. Only later did I realize she had over heard me. Hardly able to contain her response, after patiently waiting for me to tearfully ask her, she exclaimed, "I will! I would! I do!"

Because Becky's siblings were all in the States, on furlough from Papua New Guinea, we decided to marry within a short period of time so they could be with us to celebrate. Besides, there was no reason to go through a long period of getting to know each other better. We had been through the most intense kind of preparation for marriage that any couple might experience. We knew each other far better than probably ninety-nine percent of people who stand before a preacher or a justice of the peace on a wedding day. We knew each other in the bad and the good, and we knew each other in the ups and the downs. It made every bit of sense in the world that we would marry and not have to undergo a long waiting period.

Our wedding day was August 10, 1996. My family and Becky's family were all very excited for us. Becky's father was very supportive. This was his little girl, and like every father, and especially every Christian father, he wanted only the best for his daughter, both emotionally and spiritually. "This marriage is a gift from the Lord," he said in his Southern twang, a twinkle in his eye.

Some of my close friends at church, however, had a more difficult time with our decision. Their mindset was clear: "How dare you not grieve longer?" I understood their concerns; after all, many of them loved

Debbie intensely and admired our relationship together as something beautiful and special. I did not fault them. Nonetheless, I was also convinced we were doing the right thing.

It is important not to cause one's brother or sister to stumble, but that does not mean we simply allow our decisions to be determined by everyone else in our life. To cause someone else to stumble means to cause that person to fall into sin. Though some of our church friends did not agree with our decision to marry quickly, I could not see how our choice would cause any of them to fall into sin. So, we did our best to help them understand and then we simply had to live with the knowledge that some people close to us thought we were moving too abruptly.

It is always wise to listen to godly counsel, but in the end you have to follow God and go with your heart. Those are the two most important criteria in decision making. The first of those, following God, takes faith and commitment and often a good dose of humility. The second, going with the heart, often requires courage. Faith and courage are two pretty good qualities for any leader to have. I can't imagine a leader being without either one of them, hopefully in pretty equal proportion.

Interestingly, though, the people in our disability ministry were unanimously ecstatic. These generally reclusive, minimally educated, "unlovely" folks were simply and wonderfully inspiring people. They had been part of our life and ministry together for several years, and God always spoke to me through what I witnessed in their lives as they dealt with some of the most difficult kinds of suffering and pain. They knew that life is short.

Though they loved Debbie deeply, they also knew we all have to find a way spiritually to resolve the challenges that are thrown in our paths. They understood the truth that "each day has enough trouble of its own" (Matthew 6:34). Therefore, don't worry about tomorrow and live each day for the Lord, following the course of action laid out for you and recognizing that one person cannot judge another's actions if they are not sinful (Romans 14:1-12). And always remember, "Each of us will give an account of himself to God" (Romans 14:12). At the judgment seat of Christ, we will be responsible for our own behavior, not that of others. The apostle Paul assures us we will all receive what is due us (2 Corinthians 5:10). Our decisions are *our* decisions, and we should make them carefully and advisedly. But we each have to choose our own course.

So, Becky and I had a new set of complications to add to our life together. We had to deal with criticisms from those close to us about our decision to marry only six months after Debbie's death. We certainly did not ask for that problem, but we should have anticipated it. And yet, in the end, that, too, was only a relatively small matter. These days we don't really hear much about that at all.

Our wedding day was picture-perfect. Many from our ministry to the disabled were there, and so were many special friends. Two guests in particular stood out prominently, quietly and courageously. Debbie's father and mother sat near the front row.

We had decided to honeymoon in Florida at my parents' condo. But only a few days later I came down with heatstroke and walking pneumonia. In addition I caught a virus. Talk about triple whammy! That was not exactly the way I wanted to start my new marriage, and it brought up shades of memory of the illness issues Debbie and I faced on our honeymoon. But the 105-degree fever and chills in our honeymoon bed turned out only to be a bump in the road. Becky suggests that my body simply realized it now had a chance to be sick—and did so. There is probably a lot of truth in that observation.

In that first year of marriage we did many fun things together, enjoying our new-found freedom and love. We made a backpacking trip out west to the Rocky Mountains and the Grand Canyon. When something reminded us of Debbie, we would always cherish the memory together and speak of her with love. Sometimes the laughter included a few tears, but they were mostly tears of joy.

It was an amazing thing to be married to a wife who was so much a positive part of my first marriage. I am not going to say we have never had any difficulty in working through our former roles as employer and employee, even "older brother"/"younger sister" or navigating through the memories of the place Debbie once held in my life. But what has helped us in that transition is that Becky also made a vital contribution to my earlier life. She is now the lady of my life, and I love her with all my heart. Now opportunities for growth in each of our walks with God abound. Becky and I are different in heritage, upbringing, personality, temperament, and even age. She's the creative butterfly, I'm the analytical anchor. She grew up in the jungle, away from urban civilization, and I've spent my career in corporate America as an executive. Yet we have so much in common.

One special thing happened to us that was a tribute to Debbie and her legacy. I led a construction team on a Joni and Friends missions trip to Ghana and we built a wheelchair distribution and repair center. I was able to take Debbie's wheelchair and I donated that to the people of Africa. My experience with my wife led me to many other opportunities to minister to disabled people, especially during the final years of her life and in the years that followed. God eventually gave me the grace to minister to many suffering people, whereas early on in our experience it was enough just to try helping my beloved wife.

I believe with all my heart that strength is given to the willing, to those who are ready to stop asking "why?" and ask instead, "what can we do now?" It was exciting to see other people get involved in disability ministry. People who never saw themselves doing such a thing found great joy in serving God in this way. Often we don't discover God's spiritual gifts to us until we have an opportunity to serve in a way we never dreamed of. Likewise, we sometimes don't find those gifts until we are forced to face the challenge of dealing with suffering, hoping God can and will make a difference in our lives and in the lives of others through us.

The trial of fire in Debbie's temporal suffering was exactly what it took for us to be drawn into an eternal relationship with God. Our momentary troubles, though overwhelming while in their midst, will be far outweighed by the eternal weight of glory that awaits us (2 Corinthians 4:17). If the glory of God can be revealed in our suffering, then the firing process of heat our physical jars of clay endure is worth the pain. God's intent is that now through the church his manifold wisdom would be made known to the rulers and authorities in the heavens (Ephesians 3:10). And often, God makes that known to those rulers through the ordeal of fire faced by his people. That fire bakes this precious clay of which our lives are formed, making us strong so we can face even more tribulation to come. It is such precious clay because it is made in the Lord's image and because we are shaped into that image by God's grace.

My business grew dramatically in the late 1990s and afterward. Eventually I became the sole owner of the company, and God blessed us in ways I could have never dreamed. The church we were apart of was in process of resurrection. My marriage was in a state of bliss—even more bliss I imagine than the playwright Aristophanes had ever even dreamed of. And on top of that, the Lord gave us two special little gifts—Debbiegrace and Emmajoy.

When God gave us our first child, Becky agreed wholeheartedly to honor Debbie's memory, and so we named our first daughter Debbiegrace. Then came Emmajoy. They both remind me of the enabling grace of God and the joy he gives if we simply live for the Lord. As they grew and began to walk and talk, they came to know Debbie's parents, Bill and Florence, as "Grammy" and "Grampy." We think of Debbie's parents as an important part of our larger family, and we hope they will always see our beautiful girls as an important part of their life.

What a thrill it was to witness the miracle of their births! I had never before wept such intense tears of joy. Every day is a continued miracle of understanding who the girls are. It is like unwrapping a gift to be able to see his handiwork demonstrated in their young lives. I can see so much of myself and Becky in them, and yet they are also who they are—precious souls and precious clay in the hands of God. They constantly remind me of the fact that my life is blessed by God, and yet this is true of all who have experienced the salvation that comes from Jesus (Ephesians 1:3-5.) It reminds me what a wise philosopher once said about love, that it never divides but only multiplies. What an incredibly beautiful truth.

As I watch my daughters in the act of worshipping God, I recall that if we come to him as a child—realizing as children do that everything we have is a gift—that we will experience that same love and affection from him that we bestow on our children, and even much more so.

Emmajoy loves to pretend she is asleep when I go to pray with her at night, and then as I pray over her sleeping form she loves to roar loudly, taking me by surprise. Recently as she pretended once more, I decided to be the first to roar—only to find she really was asleep. I spooked her silly! What a delightful blessing my girls are to me now, exceeding my expectations and even my wildest dreams as a dad in his fifties!

When Debbiegrace was born, and again with some more help from our friend Kara, who had written the "smile poem" that so blessed both Becky and me, I wrote these words to her:

What's in a Name?

Our precious little bundle
As we look into your pretty face,
We cannot help but be reminded
Of God's abundant, loving grace.

Grace—the very name you bear
We pray you'll someday grasp,
The full extent of all it means
In present as in past.

As you begin your life with us
We want to fill you in,
On how God has brought us to this point
With the past, we will begin.

Your Dad, when he was younger,
Before your Mom he knew,
Fell in love with Debbie
They were married, too.

What a special lady Debbie was
Her smile lit her whole sweet face.
Even when she got real sick
She shared it everyplace.

God used her sickness for His Glory
As only He can do.
Both Dad and Debbie came to know Him
In that trial He walked them through.

Your Mom and Deb became best friends
Mom gave her loving care.
Both Mom and Dad now have those memories
With Debbie that they share.

So God in His great mercy
Knew Debbie was in pain,
And took her home to be with Him
Now Heaven is her gain.

Though Mom and Dad both feel their loss
They rejoice for Debbie too.
She's with her Savior face to face
A body whole and new.

While in that time of sorrow,
God's special plan unwound.
He drew Mom and Dad together
In love they now abound.

We'll never really understand
All of God's great plan.
But Debbiegrace, one thing's for sure,
It's all been from His loving Hand.

So that Debbie—also is your name
And now you know the reason.
Debbie was so much a part
Of that unforgotten season.

We don't dare try to just forget
This unique and special story.
To do so would rob our great God
Of all His rightful glory.

Now, Debbiegrace, your Mom and Dad
Promise you today
To raise you in the truth of God
So you'll learn His Way.

We hardly even know you yet
But look forward as you grow
To watch you learn of Jesus
And how He loves you so.

We commit to love each other
In a home that's stable,
But we can only promise this
Because we know He's able.

"Debbiegrace"—what's in a name?
Just letters to be spoken?
Not yours, my precious 'Bayber'
It's God's reminder token.

Two years later God gave us another just as special gift, my daughter Emmajoy.

Emmajoy

It was just the three of us before you came around
Mommy, Daddy, Debbiegrace—by love we were bound
then Mommy started getting sick and knew you are on the way
she craved odd things like pickle juice—even sardines were okay!

Your sister Debbiegrace looked forward to seeing you
she sang you "Jesus loves me," and felt you kicking too.
On the 30th of April you came early by three weeks—
perfectly formed, light blue eyes, and little cute red cheeks.

We named you Joy by faith, you know—your first four months were tough.
Colicky and spitting up—those times for you and mom were rough.
But sure enough just like in life when trials come our way
you started feeling better and began smiling every day.

That smile radiates so much on you our dear sweet child,
Grandma and Grandpa have been known to say your forehead even smiles!
When Daddy comes home from his work after a long and tiring day
one thing he can always count on—your smile for him in your special way!

You're a laid-back little girl, your sweet temperament is mild
you are a little snuggler—how we love our precious child!
When you giggle from the pit of your tummy we laugh, too.
And lately you're found growling like a lion in the zoo.

Although you've only been with us for a little less than a year
Emmajoy—there's no way around it—to us you are so dear.
You are another blessing from Jesus whom we serve and love
we truly see you as a joy and a special guest from God above.

We cannot see what's ahead and the future we don't know
but one thing we will promise as we watch you learn and grow:
we will teach you about Jesus, and follow God in training you
and pray you'll come to know Him and love Him as we do.

The Glory of God

I lived with my new family in the home that I had designed and built for Debbie for a few more years. Although I could have never imagined ever leaving that house, it became clear that we needed to. So we did. One more difficult yet necessary lesson in realizing that we are mere sojourners. The things of this world must be held ever so loosely.

My life is so full. Certainly I must be the most blessed man on the planet. When I read the story of Job, I can't help but identify in a small way with some of the trials he went through. He suffered much more than we did, and he had many very beautiful things taken from him. And yet, at the end of the story, he was given more in return than he ever lost.

Unfortunately, your story will probably also include suffering in some form or another along the line. This is a reality on which we can always count. The apostle John reminded us that Jesus said, "In this world you will have tribulation" (John 16:33). But remember also that Jesus added to that comment when he said, "Be courageous! I have overcome the world." Be assured that as you place your trust in him who has endured the ultimate suffering, Christ will lift you above your circumstances in his Holy Spirit and enable you also to be an overcomer.

As I look back, the suffering we endured together was a very important part of our spiritual and emotional development. Even now, as suffering comes to us in different forms, I'm tempted to think, "Your problems are nothing compared to ours." It is probably normal for us to compare our suffering with that of others enduring pain and sorrow. I still remember Debbie's "small potatoes." But Debbie's suffering, like all our sufferings, was only relative. Others have suffered, some even more than Debbie, and some much less. But this is not to be our focus. Nothing can compare to the sufferings of Christ, who endured all things for the joy set before him (Hebrews 12:2). His sufferings stand alone because he endured more than mere physical pain. In his sacrifice for humanity he took our sin upon himself and received the outpouring of God's just wrath in our place.

Life is so rich in every imaginable way for us—a mere reflection, though, of all God has planned for our eternal existence. Never will I forget the blessing given to our family by God through Debbie, my Precious Beeba. She was a window God's light showed through. Such precious clay. I long to again to see her smiling face singing with a restored voice, running with restored legs, and yes even dancing the ultimate waltz with her Savior and King in the new heavens and new earth.

I am confident Debbie and I, along with Becky, Debbiegrace and Emmajoy, and hopefully along with you, can look forward to an eternity in fellowship with the great Bridegroom of the church, our Lord Jesus Christ, and an eternity of glorious bliss. Till then we too, like you, will be given God's grace to meet our challenges. To him alone be the praise and glory and honor for this story. It is his story, not one we conjured up or could have even imagined. My prayer is that you also have genuinely become one "born from above" and part of his redemption story. He alone is worthy!

Along with You…In His Eternal Grip of Love,
Mark

Meet the Author

MARK GRAWEHR BEGAN work in the construction trade in 1971, incorporated his first business in 1978, and in 1979 completed a B.S. degree with honors in mechanical engineering from Newark College of Engineering. He carries multiple construction credentials and trade licenses, and is a licensed professional engineer in several states.

Under Grawehr's leadership his Trimech Corporation became a renowned engineering, construction, facilities operations and service company. In 2001, recognizing the synergy offered through a formal affiliation with an even larger corporation, he sold Trimech and enabled it to become part of a Fortune 500 company. Mark continued to operate the business as company president and senior vice president of the parent company until transitioning to full time ministry in May, 2006.

Just after Mark married in 1979, his wife Debbie was severely stricken with MS. Within about a year they were drawn to faith in Jesus Christ through this trial and then became involved in disability ministry. Debbie was paralyzed, legally blind, and unable to speak for the duration of almost their entire marriage before passing away at the age of thirty-eight in February 1996.

Mark has served in various church and parachurch ministries in both fiduciary and pastoral capacities of leadership since 1987. He recently completed his master's degree at Alliance Theological Seminary and became ordained. He is currently serving as a pastor at a local church and is completing a Doctorate of Biblical Studies. Mark's ongoing entrepreneurial endeavors enable him to serve freely as he pursues his life mission—to make a significant difference in the advancement of God's Kingdom through effective, Christ-centered leadership.

Today Mark and his wife Becky are the parents of two homeschooled daughters, Debbiegrace and Emmajoy. They live in New Jersey.

SALES OF *SUCH PRECIOUS CLAY*

All proceeds from the sale of this book will be given in memory of
Debbie Grawehr to Joni and Friends International Disability Center,
and will be used for the benefit of people with disabilities.

Visit Author's Website:
www.preciousclayministries.org